BUILDING A DELIBERATIVE DEMOCRACY

An evaluation of two citizens' juries

by Marian Barnes

INSTITUTE FOR PUBLIC POLICY RESEARCH

INSTITUTE FOR PUBLIC POLICY RESEARCH

30-32 Southampton St
London WC2E 7RA
Tel: 0171 470 6100
Fax: 0171 470 6111
ippr@easynet.co.uk
www.ippr.org.uk
Registered charity 800065

The Institute for Public Policy Research is an independent charity whose purpose is to contribute to public understanding of social, economic and political questions through research, discussion and publication. It was established in 1988 by leading figures in the academic, business and trade-union communities to provide an alternative to the free market think tanks.

IPPR's research agenda reflects the challenges facing Britain and Europe. Current programmes cover the areas of economic and industrial policy, Europe, governmental reform, human rights, defence, social policy, the environment and media issues.

Besides its programme of research and publication, IPPR also provides a forum for political and trade union leaders, academic experts and those from business, finance, government and the media, to meet and discuss issues of common concern.

Trustees

Production & design by **EMPHASIS**
Printed and bound in Great Britain by Biddles Ltd, Guildford and King's Lynn
ISBN 1 86030 087 1
© IPPR 1999

Contents

Acknowledgements

My thanks to the participants of the two juries: jurors, witnesses, commissioners and facilitators, for tolerating my presence and responding to my questions. Thanks to Clare Delap of IPPR for providing me with all the background information and for being an interested, but independent evaluation commissioner. Thanks to Clare and Anna Coote for useful comments on a draft report and for stimulating further thinking. Thanks to Corinne Wales both for helping with the data collection and for insightful comments on a draft report. I hope the result is of interest and value to all those interested in renewing democratic practice.

About the author

Marian Barnes is Director of Social Research in the Department of Social Policy and Social Work at the University of Birmingham. She has been involved in research and development relating to user involvement and public participation for 13 years and has published widely in this area. Recent publications include *Care, Communities and Citizens* (Longman), *Paths to Empowerment* with Lorna Warren (Policy Press) and *The People'ss Health Service?* (The NHS Confederation).

Summary

Citizens' juries and citizen participation

Citizens' juries are one among a number of new approaches to democratic practice being developed throughout the public sector. These are intended to enable deliberation amongst citizens and between citizens and 'experts' as a means of promoting informed citizen participation in issues of public policy. The development of such new forms of democratic practice has led to calls for the various models and methods to be evaluated. This in turn has resulted in a need for models of evaluation appropriate to learning about both the process and the outcomes of deliberation in different forums. Such evaluation needs to be capable of reflecting the values of democracy and social justice which citizen participation is intended to promote, as well as to answer questions about the comparative merits of different models and the effectiveness with which models are implemented in practice. The evaluation reported here was intended to contribute to learning about evaluation in this context as well as to provide substantive learning about the two citizens' juries which were the subject of study. It was designed to answer questions about:

- The characteristics of those taking part in the juries.

- The impact of the process on those acting as witnesses.

- The nature of the deliberative process and its impact on the jurors themselves.

- The impact of the juries on policy making and on citizenship.

The two juries

The two juries which were the subject of this evaluation were very different from one another. One was commissioned by the Eastern Health and Social Services Board and the Eastern Health and Social Services Council in Northern Ireland and was intended to enable citizens to reflect on proposed health service changes contained in a consultation paper: 'Fit for the Future'. It was the first citizens' jury held in Northern Ireland and took place in August 1998 in the context of continuing debate about constitutional changes following on from the Good Friday agreement. The other jury was commissioned by the Millennium Debate of the Age as part of a series of public consultations about a broad spectrum of policy issues relevant to the needs of an ageing population. It was unusual in that the jurors were young people aged 15-16. The jury sat for two and a half days rather than the four days of the Belfast jury. It took place in Swansea, although the issues under discussion – the design of the built environment – were not intended to be specific to that location.

The jurors

Jurors were selected to match population profiles drawn up for each area. Most of those taking part considered that the jurors represented a cross-section of people living in their area. All jurors in both juries were white since the population profiling had indicated that less than one black juror would be included amongst the 16 people in each jury. None of the jurors was disabled and the Belfast jury did not include anyone over 70.

Jurors' reasons for accepting the invitation to take part reflect a range of motivations. Most were pleased to be invited and were glad their ideas were being sought. They saw the juries as an opportunity to have their say and in Belfast in particular also as a learning opportunity. The young people saw it as something to do and an opportunity to meet new people. The fee for taking part was a particularly significant factor for the young people, but was also a factor affecting decisions of the adult jurors to take part.

The process of deliberation

Deliberation took place in both plenary and small groups sessions. Since the small group sessions were intended to provide an opportunity for unobserved discussion to take place, the only direct observation of such sessions was on the third day of the Belfast jury. By this time the jurors were comfortable with the process and largely unaware of being observed. The level of involvement of jurors in plenary discussion was very varied in both juries. There were four jurors in the Belfast jury who made very few contributions to the discussion, one of whom made no input in plenary session at all. Three of these four jurors were the youngest members of the jury. Similarly there was a considerable range in the level of input amongst the Swansea jurors. In this case five of the six making the most frequent contributions were young women.

The dynamics of the deliberative process were different in each jury. In Swansea the process often had the characteristics of a question and answer session, with the facilitators seeking to engage jurors by asking them questions which prompted little debate. There was one occasion when the young people did engage in interested and active deliberation, with different views being expressed and explored. However, the topic of this discussion was tangential to the focus of the session and when the facilitator brought them back to focus on the topic debate died down. The young people drew to some extent on their own experiences in contributing to discussion, but there was comparatively little use of witness evidence in deliberation amongst themselves in plenary.

The deliberative process in Belfast can be considered more successful. Whilst jurors regarded the witnesses as having varying degrees of usefulness to their deliberations, it was evident that they were drawing on both witness input and personal experience in considering the topics under discussion. Personal experience was used to question witness evidence as well as a resource in its own right. Deliberation amongst jurors was lively with the facilitator acting to clarify, summarise or move things on, rather than to prompt discussion. Certain of the jurors themselves also took on the roles of clarifying, distinguishing different points being made and suggesting ways through disagreement. Jurors sometimes engaged with very detailed and complex issues, although this may at some points have been at the expense of a more strategic picture.

Responses of jurors to the jury process were largely positive, although some of the Swansea jurors were less enthusiastic. Although the Swansea jury was shorter than the Belfast jury the young people were more likely to consider that the process had lasted too long. A number of the Belfast jurors considered that they had had insufficient time adequately to get to grips with the issues they were debating. Most felt that the process had enabled different views to be expressed and be reflected in the final report. However, there were also suggestions that the imperative to produce a report by the end had led to some differences remaining unexplored.

Building citizenship?

The jurors can be characterised as neither active nor alienated citizens before their involvement in the jury. Most of the Belfast jurors were regular voters in elections. Ten of the Swansea jurors and 14 of the Belfast jurors had signed a petition, two Swansea jurors had written to their local MP and two to a councillor.

Following the jury most had talked to other people who had not taken part about what had happened at the jury, and virtually a half of the jurors had talked to each other following the jury. Some had read things or watched TV programmes relevant to the jury topic and some of the Belfast jurors had attended follow up meetings of the EHSSB or the Council at which their report was being considered.

Most thought they had learnt from taking part in the jury. That learning was seen to comprise:

- new information

- increased understanding

- awareness of different views and experiences

- encouraging reflection

- learning about the process of deliberation

- the potential to achieve change.

Most thought that they would take part in a citizens' jury again if they were asked.

Responses to a question about the meaning of the term 'citizen' demonstrated that it is a term largely absent from everyday discourse. However, jurors reflected an inclusive perspective on what it means to be a citizen, with some also suggesting that it implied an active concern and preparedness to take part in some way.

The 'experts'

None of those who acted as witnesses had taken part in a citizens' jury before, although the majority had previous experiences of other forms of public participation. With one exception the Swansea witnesses reported a rather low key experience with little sense that it had involved substantial learning either for the jurors or for the witnesses. None felt threatened by the experience and none had undertaken substantial preparation in advance.

The responses of Belfast 'experts' to the invitation to be a witness were highly varied. Some were extremely enthusiastic and some reported that they were terrified by the prospect. Most prepared for their role and some described this as a process of simplifying without becoming patronising.

Some witnesses were disappointed or concerned about the limited time available for presenting their material and being questioned on it. This was reflected in a degree of uncertainty about the extent to which they or the jurors had learned from the process and in whether the experience of the jury would have any impact on the way in which they might do their jobs in future.

The impact on commissioners and policy outcomes

In neither case were the commissioners of the juries in a position to directly implement jury recommendations, apart from recommendations from the Belfast jurors about the process of citizen participation. However, both undertook to include jurors' recommendations in their reports to other bodies. In addition, consideration was being given to ways in which the Belfast jurors could be kept in touch with developments and might play a further consultative role in relation to health and social services policy.

In both cases the commissioners observed at least part of the jury process. Their responses to this were very different. The MDA commissioner was very disappointed with the way in which the jury had been conducted and with its outcome. This had not deterred her from further attempts to consult young people, but she felt that a very different process would be necessary to release young people's creativity. The EHSSB and EHSSC commissioners, in contrast, were very satisfied with what they had observed of the jury process and also thought that it had lived up to their expectations in terms of the composition of the jury. There was some question, reflecting concern by the jurors themselves, that there had been insufficient time for deliberation of the range of complex issues involved. They considered they would be likely to use a citizens' jury again, but agreed that it is a method to be used sparingly and can only constitute one element in a strategy for public participation.

Issues raised

The findings from the evaluation of these two particular juries raise issues about the model in general, as well as its application in these two cases.

Whilst it is recognised that a group of 16 people cannot be considered to comprise a representative sample of a total population, the criterion of 'fairness' which has been suggested as a key criterion by which to assess models of citizen participation implies that there should be no structured exclusions. However, the composition of the juries raises questions about whether opportunities to take part were equally distributed. No black people were selected because of the small numbers within the relevant populations. There were no disabled people involved and an equal opportunity to take part would have required appropriate attention to be given to physical access, and to methods of communication capable of including people with hearing or sight impairments. There were no frail older people involved and the four day schedule might be a systematic source of exclusion for people able to be active only for short periods.

The implications of these absences relate both to the nature of the deliberative process and the range of experiences and voices reflected within it.

The structure of a citizens' jury requires people to be categorised as 'citizens' or 'experts' because of the roles they play within the jury. But these categories are not exclusive and are open to different interpretations. 'Experts' are also citizens and, as the Belfast jury demonstrated, someone who could have been sampled as a citizen participant (the mother of a disabled child) was invited as a result of a request by jurors to give evidence as an expert witness.

Citizens' juries are seen as a way of engaging with 'ordinary citizens'. The random selection process means that anyone could be invited to participate. However, those with a particular interest in some issues, because of their experiences of chronic illness or disability, are less likely to take part. As well as being citizens they are people in danger of being socially excluded and it is particularly important that their voices are heard.

The nature of the deliberative process which developed in the Swansea jury suggests that the model was not the most appropriate way of exploring the ideas and views of young people. This may in part have been a consequence of the jury topic being defined for the participants rather than by them. Groups which rarely have their voices heard in decision-making forums are likely to be more effectively engaged when they have the opportunity to put onto the agenda for discussion issues of importance to them. Opportunities for separate debate amongst groups of citizens who share particular experiences, such as growing older or living in poverty, are important as a means of articulating perspectives on public policy which are often different from those of people occupying more powerful social positions. Nevertheless, it is also important to create opportunities for people occupying different social positions to deliberate together to create new understandings and new outcomes.

These observations emphasise the necessity for a range of opportunities to be available to enable citizens from all social groups to contribute to public policy-making. In creating such a range of opportunities it will be important to avoid the danger of a 'hierarchy of legitimacy' developing which privileges particular groups.

The experience of this evaluation suggests the following criteria for the evaluation of citizen deliberation, in addition to the criteria of fairness and competence suggested by other researchers:

- inclusiveness

- capacity to deal with difference and dissent

- the opportunity to scrutinise experts and information – including scrutiny of the definition of 'expert'

- the extent to which participants are able to developing skills and understanding

- producing an outcome.

None of these criteria can be assessed by means of simple tick box analysis. Further study of citizen participation and the outcomes it can produce may be best understood as requiring research rather than evaluation.

1. Citizens' juries and citizen participation

New approaches to citizen participation are being developed from within many different spheres of public policy making and public service delivery. At the same time, new forms of politics have emerged among culturally diverse social movements, and established political parties concerned about disenchantment with mainstream politics, are seeking different ways of legitimising their positions. Increasing inequalities of wealth and opportunity have led to excluded sections of the population feeling disenfranchised. Action from within public institutions to encourage greater citizen participation is taking place alongside action among those excluded from mainstream decision making, seeking to have their voices heard. The tasks of social, economic and democratic regeneration are inter-linked and are explicitly so in initiatives such as community planning, action to address health inequalities in Health Action Zones, and partnerships with communities to deliver the objectives of the Single Regeneration Budget.

In this context citizens' juries are just one example of the new approaches to democratic practice which are being developed throughout the public sector. They are intended to access the 'ordinary wisdom' of the public in the development of public policy (Davies et al, 1998), and can be considered as a practical expression of the notion of discursive or deliberative democracy (see Dryzek, 1990, Gutman and Thompson, 1997). Gutman and Thompson identify three principles underpinning deliberative democracy: reciprocity, publicity and accountability, and describe the overall purpose as to 'promote extensive moral argument about the merits of public policies in public forums, with the aim of reaching provisional moral agreement and maintaining mutual respect among citizens'.

Citizens' juries were developed in the US and in Germany (where they are known as planning cells). They were introduced into the UK in the early 1990s and were originally taken up by local authorities and health authorities as a means of consulting the public on issues involving a choice between specific policy options, such as what model of palliative care to develop (Walsall Health Authority), or broader questions, such as how the harmful impact of drug taking on individuals and communities might be reduced (London Borough of Lewisham). Subsequently juries have been commissioned by other agencies in both the public and private sector (see, for example, Dunkerley and Glasner, 1998). Their development in the UK has been supported and evaluated by two research and policy units: the King's Fund and the Institute for Public Policy Research (IPPR), and by the Local Government Management Board and the School of Public Policy at the University of Birmingham.

The practice of citizens' juries has been described in some detail elsewhere (Coote and Lenaghan, 1997, Crosby, 1995, Stewart *et al*, 1994). Briefly, they have the following characteristics:

- They involve a random sample of citizens, who have been selected to participate, rather than having themselves having taken the initiative to become involved.

- They normally focus on a particular question which requires value choices to be made in developing public policy.

- Deliberation is facilitated in the following ways: firstly by the presentation of evidence by 'experts'[1] in ways which are accessible to 'non-experts' and the opportunity for citizens to question experts on this evidence, and secondly, by being moderated by facilitators who are independent of those who commissioned the jury and who have no particular stake in the outcome.

- The aims are to develop the expression of more informed views on the part of the citizens involved, to develop deliberation among citizens in order to reach an overall view on the issue under discussion.

- The conclusions from citizens' juries are brought to bear upon the policy-making process, to improve the quality of decisions. It is intended that the outcomes of deliberation will inform policy and good practice requires an obligation on the part of jury commissioners to respond to the jurors' report. However, there is no necessary requirement that jurors' recommendations will be accepted by the commissioning authority nor by any other authority who might be affected by the recommendations made.

This report is the result of an evaluation commissioned by IPPR of two juries conducted during the summer of 1998. The evaluation was intended to contribute to learning about the role citizens' juries might play in revitalising democratic practice and enabling public participation in processes of public policy making. It was also intended to pilot a method of evaluating deliberative involvement exercises such as citizens' juries in order to try to produce criteria for their success.

Evaluating citizen participation

The evaluation of citizen participation requires the application of evaluation models appropriate to this learning objective (Barnes et al, 1997). Evaluation in this context has to recognise the political nature of the participative process and reflect in the way the evaluation itself is conducted the importance of enabling different voices to be heard. Evaluators are citizens as well as researchers (Greene, 1996) and evaluation can contribute to or frustrate the cause of democracy and social justice to which citizen participation is intended to contribute (House, 1993).

Models of evaluation have been developed in the context of public policy which aim to reflect the contested and dynamic nature of the process of policy making and implementation (for example, Barnes, 1993, Finne et al, 1995). Such models emphasise the importance of evaluation as a process of learning rather than judging (Rebien, 1996, Stewart and Walsh, 1994). Evaluation questions are couched in terms of 'what are the conditions for success?' and 'why/how has this initiative been successful (or not)?' rather than solely by reference to the measurement of previously specified objectives. The design of such evaluations aims to enable learning among those actively engaged in the programme which is the subject of evaluation. When the subject of evaluation is itself a process intended to enable marginalised or excluded groups to play a part in decision making (as, for example, in the case of community development), then engaging participants in evaluating both the process and outcomes of such activity is integral to the achievement of overall objectives (Voluntary Activity Unit, 1997).

Evaluating processes and outcomes

Involving citizens in decision-making processes is intended to make a difference to the outcomes of those decisions. But involvement has other objectives as well, not least that of creating more informed citizens who are better able to deliberate on issues of public policy. In this as in many other cases the outcome of participation cannot be separated from the process by which people are enabled to become involved. Means and ends are inextricably linked. The question 'what are the conditions for success?' requires an analysis and understanding of the way in which any initiative is undertaken and how this relates to the impact it has.

The process of enabling people to take part has the potential to create change in the participants before there is any observable change in the policies or services produced as a result. For example, carers who became involved in panels to support and review a programme of developments deriving from earlier consultations about community care services expressed some frustration at the slow pace of change. But they also recognised that their involvement in the process could be considered an outcome in its own right because it marked an acceptance of their expert knowledge as a significant factor in decision making (Barnes and Wistow, 1993). Conversely, if taking part makes no difference to the citizens who have been involved, if they are not in some way changed by the process or do not change the process itself, then it is hard to see how it can be considered to have been a success. In situations in which policy or service outcomes are uncertain and may take some time to realise, the intrinsic benefits of participation are likely to be important to make it worth people's while to take part. And if a key objective is the creation of a healthier, more active democracy, then the way in which the practice of participation is implemented should itself be the subject of analysis to assess whether or not it meets criteria of democratic participation.

Any evaluation of public participation must thus consider the process by which involvement is secured, its capacity to provide direct and positive impacts on participants, and whether this represents a significant change in decision making processes, consistent with the values of democracy and social justice. This requires an analysis of the processes by which participation is secured, and of who is included in those processes.

Gastil (1993) has considered the process of democracy as it operates within small groups:

> A small group is democratic if it has equally distributed
> decision-making power, an inclusive membership committed

to democracy, healthy relationships among its members, and a democratic method of deliberation. Group deliberation is democratic if group members have equal and adequate opportunities to speak, neither withhold information nor verbally manipulate one another, and are able and willing to listen (p6)

An evaluation of citizens' juries needs to include an assessment of their capacity to meet the conditions outlined by Gastil. In her evaluation of citizens' juries commissioned by Health Authorities McIver (1997) recorded information about the environment in which juries were held, the process by which the juries were conducted, including the order of events and how long was spent on each part of the process, the content of discussions and observations of jurors' moods, the nature of the questions asked and the way in which deliberation was progressing. McIver's evaluation and that conducted by Stewart and Hall of juries commissioned by local authorities (LGMB, 1996) have started to address the extent to which the jury process, the methods of facilitation used, the way in which witnesses were asked to present their cases, and the balance between full group and small group discussions, enabled informed deliberation to develop. They have also sought to consider whether the process itself is biased – either as a result of its conceptual base, or because of the way the process is run. This current evaluation has sought to develop this aspect of the evaluation process (see Chapters 3 and 4).

Citizens' juries are intended to provide a forum for collective deliberation which is inclusive of any citizen. Phillips (1993 and 1995) and Young (1990) have considered the significance of deliberative processes for hearing different voices, particularly those most likely to be unheard or excluded – women, people from different minority ethnic groups, people living in poverty – and enabling participants to reflect on their own ideas as a result. Young (quoted in Phillips, 1993, p158) writes:

group representation unravels the false consensus that cultural imperialism may have produced, and reveals group bias in norms, standards, styles and perspectives that have been assumed as universal or of highest value. By giving voice to formerly silenced or devalued needs and experiences, group representation forces participants in discussion to take a reflective distance on their assumptions and think beyond their own interests. When confronted with interests, needs and opinions that derived from very different social positions and experience, persons sometimes come to understand the limitations of their own experience and perspective for coming to conclusions about the best policy for everyone.

'Presence' (Phillips, 1995) is necessary for voices to be expressed. Deliberation is necessary for reflection on the significance of different positions and experiences in reaching decisions which have the capacity to respond to cultural diversity and inequality. But the process of deliberation may itself need to vary if this is to be an inclusive process. For example, processes for encouraging deliberation among young people may need to be different from those involved in encouraging deliberation among adults; 'dialogue' *per se* can exclude people who are hard of hearing unless provision is made to enable this; methods which are effective for enabling people with learning difficulties to express their views draw on forms of representation other than language; while deliberation in an ethnically-diverse community may require the use of interpreters.

Webler (1995) has developed what he calls an 'evaluative yardstick' for the purpose of assessing whether models of citizen participation meet criteria of competence and fairness in deliberation. While Armour (1995) has applied this 'in principle' to the citizens' jury model, it is not clear that this has led to an 'in practice' application to any specific jury. Nor does this yardstick directly address the questions posed above about their capacity to include different groups. The normative nature of the criteria proposed by Webler to evaluate deliberation – competence and fairness – could be construed as requiring communication skills which are unequally shared between different groups within the population. He recognises the potential difficulty:

> Except for the most obvious cases of mental illness and the inability to use language (and even here it is sometimes difficult to draw a clear line), excluding participation opportunities based on assessments of individuals' cognitive competence is

unethical. Even lingual incompetence in the dominant language is not an excuse to legitimately exclude [sic] a citizen – translators should be hired. (Webler, 1995, p55)

The general criteria of fairness and competence are important in assessing whether citizens' juries meet their declared objectives. But the question of how competent and fair discourse can be enabled among diverse groups of citizens raises a further criterion to be used in evaluating citizens' jurors and other methods of citizen participation: that of inclusiveness. One of the empirical questions to be answered is whether any single method of participation (other than voting) is capable of a comprehensive inclusiveness, or whether the criterion of fairness requires the use of diverse methods to enable participation.

Different models of public participation have different purposes and aim to hear the voices of different categories of citizens (see Barnes, 1997, IHSM, NHSE, and NHS Confederation, 1998). For example, initiatives which are intended to enable citizens who are also users or potential users of particular services, or who are directly affected by particular policies, usually seek to improve the responsiveness of those services as a result of involving users in decision making about service or policy design (see Barnes and Bennet, 1997, Beresford and Harding, 1993).

Citizens' juries are intended to impact on the specific policy issues which are the subject of deliberation, and have broader purposes related to the development of a more participatory democracy. In her evaluation of juries commissioned by Health Authorities McIver considered the immediate response of the Health Authorities to the jury recommendations. She looked at issues such as the time period within which a response was made, the forum in which juries' recommendations were considered, whether the juries were considered to have introduced new ideas to the decision making process, and the nature of the response made to the juries' recommendations. She found that jury recommendations had influenced decision making, although mainly by 'adding weight' to issues and thus giving them higher priority, rather than by suggesting radical alternatives.

Assessing the direct impact of juries on those who commissioned them is important, not least because this will affect their continuing to use citizens' juries or other deliberative methods as part of an overall strategy for developing public participation. As Armour (1995) notes in her analysis of citizens' juries based on the evaluation framework proposed by Webler (ibid) 'As to the merits of the citizens' juries recommendations and the degree of influence the jury process has had on decision-making processes, there is a noticeable lack of research which would enable any assessment to be made. This is unfortunate because, without such assessments, the model is likely to remain "unique" rather than a standard approach to public involvement' (p185). She goes on to argue that one of the limitations of the citizens' jury model as implemented to date in the US is that policy makers are not active participants in the process. It does not impact on processes by which public officials are required to give account and be challenged on their decisions and action. This observation reinforces the earlier argument about the link between process and outcome. Impact on policy makers is more likely if they are involved with citizens in the deliberative process itself. To some extent this has been the case with citizens' juries conducted in the UK and this is one topic considered in this report of the evaluation of two juries. There is potential for officials as well as citizens to gain from more participative approaches to decision making and there is empirical evidence to suggest that officials do value and learn from engaging in dialogue with users and citizens (Barnes and Bennet 1998, Harrison et al, 1997).

For public service officials as well as for citizens the service and policy outcomes of participation are uncertain, not least because of the multiplicity of factors which will influence those outcomes. I have suggested above that this implies that participation must provide intrinsic benefits if people are to be motivated to take part. Participation must provide value *per se* to participants – both citizens and officials. For citizens that value will often consist of:

- increased knowledge, understanding or information;

- enhanced capacities to engage in deliberation;

- an enhanced sense of self-esteem and self-worth deriving from the knowledge that your views and knowledge are valued;

- benefits deriving from the social contact, friendship and support offered by collective organisation or action.

For officials, organisational learning and improved public confidence and legitimacy are likely to be important. Some have also talked of the enjoyment that comes from engaging directly with local people and the renewed sense of commitment to their work. These intrinsic benefits can also be considered outcomes or impacts of participation.

The overall conclusion from this analysis is that evaluation of citizens' juries and any other method of public participation must focus on the process by which people are enabled to take part in its own right. This includes questions of who takes part and who does not take part – the 'inclusiveness' criterion, what happens during the course of deliberation, and what impact taking part in the process as a whole has on all those involved, including those commissioning the jury, those giving evidence to it, and the citizens who take part as jurors. Assessment of the policy impact is also important, but, as is shown in Chapter 2, can often be much more difficult to achieve within a realistic time frame.

2. The two juries

The two citizens' juries which were the subject of this evaluation were very different from each other. While one of the juries was typical of a number that have taken place previously in England, the other was an experiment in applying the model to a targeted sub-group of the population – young people aged 15-16.

The first jury took place in Belfast. It was commissioned by the Eastern Health and Social Services Board (EHSSB) and the Eastern Health and Social Services Council (EHSSC – the equivalent of a Community Health Council in England) to explore citizens' views about proposals for the re-organisation of health services in Northern Ireland. These were published in a consultation paper 'Fit for the Future'. The 'charge' to the jury (as it is known in the US) focused on three questions underpinning a wide-ranging set of proposals contained within the consultation paper. These were:

- What do we want from our health and personal social services? What can be done to make them better?

- What are the advantages and disadvantages of a move to primary care groups.[2] How can our concerns be met?

- Should the public be involved in making decisions about health and personal social services, to what extent, and if so how?

The jury took place over one evening and four days in the summer of 1998.

The second was commissioned by the Millennium Debate of the Age (MDA) as part of a programme of events intended both to raise public awareness about the implications of a substantial change in the age profile of the population, and to explore citizens' views about the way a range of public policies should respond to this shift. The MDA is concerned to examine the views of citizens of all ages about these issues and they have commissioned juries involving people of different age groups as part of the overall programme. The jury which formed the subject of this study involved a group of 15-16 year olds in Swansea. While it was held in Swansea, the issues which were the subject of deliberation were not specific to that location. Jurors were asked to reflect on the nature of urban environments in the context of an ageing population. The precise questions put to the jurors were:

- What are the most important physical features of a neighbourhood?

- What are the most important things to bear in mind when we are planning new neighbourhoods?

- What kinds of neighbourhoods do we want in the future?

This jury was shorter than is typically the case for adult juries. It took place over one evening and two day sessions in the summer of 1998.

The similarity between the two juries was that neither required jurors to reach a specific decision about policy or service development options. Rather they were designed to enable exploration of views, attitudes and values which might guide decision makers in reaching decisions about a range of issues. They were thus concerned with 'deliberation' rather than 'arbitration'. This is very different from the health service juries supported by the King's Fund and other juries held by local and health authorities which were intended to assist decision makers to resolve issues where there was a clear choice to be made between specific options (New, 1998).

The scope of the evaluation

There is a distinction to be made between evaluating particular examples of a process such as a citizens' jury and drawing conclusions about such approaches to citizen participation as a whole. One jury might be considered highly successful while another might be open to considerable criticism – because of the way in which jurors were recruited, the way questions were framed or the way in which the process was facilitated, for example. Methods might be considered highly successful in their own terms, but capable only of impacting on a very small number of people directly involved in the process.

Nevertheless, a key starting point for assessing the contribution of different methods of democratic practice to overall aims of building a deliberative democracy, must be the actual practice of such initiatives themselves. Armour's evaluation of the citizens' jury model (1995) does not consider particular examples of juries in practice (other than in broad illustrative terms) and thus can only offer a perspective on the *potential* of juries to fulfil the evaluative criteria relating to the fairness and competence of discourse. In contrast, evaluations by McIver of juries focusing on health policy issues and by Hall and Stewart of juries commissioned by local authorities looked at examples of the model in practice and were able to draw conclusions about, for example, the practical issues: such as time and cost involved, as well as to make some observations about the response of commissioning authorities to jury recommendations. But neither focus on the detailed questions about the nature of the discourse which Webler (1995) has suggested is necessary to assess whether citizens' juries meet the criteria of 'fairness and competence' by which citizen participation should be judged.

Evaluative questions can be framed to address different levels and dimensions of practice. The first level questions to be asked about new methods of democratic practice are of the following type: Do they actually do what they aim to do and is this considered to be of value in its own right? If the answer to these questions is 'no', then broader questions about the place of such methods in developing democratic practice may well be irrelevant. We should, instead, be seeking alternative means of seeking the desired ends or looking for ways of improving the practice of implementing the model. If the answer to those questions is 'yes' then we should move on to posing those broader questions which cannot be answered solely by reference to the success or otherwise of particular examples of the practice. Such questions would include issues relating to the impact of such methods on the practice of democracy more generally and their place within a wider range of methods of encouraging citizen participation. Questions can also be posed about their potential to reinforce or challenge the status quo in terms both of who is involved and what are the policy outcomes.

This evaluation was conducted over a short time period – four months – with limited resources. In this context its aims were modest and findings should not be considered 'the final word' on the role and contribution of citizens' juries to democratic practice. Indeed, one aim was to pilot methods of evaluation appropriate to initiatives of this type. Many of the participative methods developed to evaluate community development and other long term initiatives in public involvement were neither feasible nor appropriate in the context of the intensive but short term process of conducting citizens' juries. At the same time, it was considered important to apply the principle of enabling participants' voices to be heard in the evaluation as well as in the juries themselves.

While the conduct of the evaluation was itself a learning process it has nevertheless produced findings of substance which can make a contribution to answering questions about the place of citizens' juries within a broader project of enhancing citizen participation, as well as reflecting on the particular experiences represented by these two, very different examples, of the method in practice.

Evaluation design and methods

The evaluation focused on these two citizens' juries as examples of the 'family' of deliberative methods of citizen involvement. The evaluation questions were framed in a way which was intended to enable exploration of characteristics that are particular to citizen's juries:

- The process is not an open one – people do not 'opt in' but are selected. How does this affect the way they feel about their participation in the process and the impact of participation on them? How does it affect their relationship with the others who have been similarly selected and the likelihood, or otherwise, of their continuing to take part in activities through which they might express their citizenship? How do those who accept the invitation to participate differ from those who decline the invitation?

- What impact does presenting evidence and being questioned on this have on the 'experts'? Do they feel threatened or stimulated by this? Do they learn from the process as well as contributing to the learning of the citizens involved? Do they become more open to engaging with citizens in decision making as a result of this experience? Does such involvement enhance their own sense of citizenship?

- Do the citizen participants become a) more informed and b) more able to engage in debate about the issue under discussion during the process? Is the process one which enables all to engage equally?

- Does being involved in the process have an impact on the way in which people think about the particular issue under discussion and issues of public policy more generally?

● Does being involved in the process have any lasting impact on people's sense of themselves as 'citizens'?

During the course of the evaluation additional questions were suggested – both by the participants and through reflection on the learning that was taking place. Jurors themselves were invited to suggest evaluation criteria and this report will reflect on these as well as on the questions posed above. At the start of the jury the Belfast jurors identified the following criteria:

● Getting results – the jury recommendations being taken up and put into action.

● Information for us.

● Good participation from everyone.

● Being clear about where there were disagreements.

● It would not necessarily involve changing your mind.

● If there were results, but the process had been boring it would still be have been worthwhile. But if it *was* boring it would mean that the facilitators had not done their job properly, and it would also mean that you wouldn't be getting involved with the process.

At the end of the jury the jurors were invited to add or amend any of these criteria. They did not want to make any amendments and once again re-iterated the importance of getting results.

The Swansea jurors were also primarily concerned that the jury should get results. One also indicated a wish for some personal recognition from the process.

The time scale of the evaluation meant that assessment of the impact of jurors' recommendations was restricted to the initial responses of commissioners and early action on receiving the jury report. However, any longer term assessment of policy impact would have been difficult to gauge in these two cases. In neither case were the commissioners of the jury in a position to reach decisions about the direct implementation of recommendations. The Belfast jury was commissioned by a Health and Social Services Board and Council in order to inform responses to the proposals for changes in health and social services set out in a recent consultation paper. While it was possible to assess the extent to which the jury had influenced the Board and Council's response to the consultative document, the final outcome – or how health and social services will be structured within Northern Ireland — was not a matter for executive action by those commissioning the jury. Indeed, any action in response to the consultation paper proposals was dependent on wider constitutional changes which were still not resolved at the time of writing. Similarly, responses to the question posed in the citizens' jury being held as part of the Millennium Debate of the Age were to be fed into a number of study groups as well as being presented to the Government and Parliamentary Select Committees. MDA itself was not in a position to act on recommendations. In both cases the commissioning bodies could guarantee only to include the outcomes of jurors' deliberations within their own recommendations to other bodies. Neither could commit themselves to take direct action in response to recommendations, with one exception (see p59-60)

The Belfast jury took place at a time when the Northern Ireland assembly was in the process of being established. It was a time of high hopes and great fears about the prospects for a constitutional resolution of the troubles. Presentation of the report coincided with the bombing in Omagh which created greater uncertainty about the constitutional settlement as well as raising particular issues about the way in which the design of health services could affect their capacity to respond to incidents such as this. It was also the first citizens' jury which had taken place in Northern Ireland. It thus appeared to have a symbolic importance which potentially went beyond the particular purposes for which it was established. Any wider impact of this jury is likely to be affected by the particular circumstances in which it was held and is unlikely to be typical of juries held in more stable political environments.

Data collection

Data were collected immediately before, during and in a period of 4-8 weeks after the juries had been conducted. Data collection focused on the direct participants: the citizens and experts involved in the process, and on those who commissioned and received the results of the jury deliberations. It did not prove possible to collect any information about those who declined the invitation to take part as jurors. In the case of the Belfast jury those who did not reply to the initial invitations had already been discounted by the time it was possible to start data collection. In the case of the Swansea jury (where recruitment methods were different), recruiters were asked to hand out questionnaires to the first 32 young people refusing the invitation. However, none of these questionnaires was returned.

The jurors were asked to complete a questionnaire concerning socio-demographic characteristics and reasons for accepting the invitation, together with some questions about previous experience of participation in other relevant activities. These were completed on the first evening of the jury itself. At this point I also invited jurors to suggest what, for them, would make the experience a worthwhile one.[3]

Both juries were observed throughout all plenary sessions, with more detailed process observation taking place at selected periods. In both juries unobserved groupwork formed an important part of the method of deliberation being pursued. In Belfast one session of groupwork was observed on the third day of the jury when jurors were used both to each other and to the procedures being adopted.

A structured schedule was developed to record observations. This was designed to record:

- the frequency of input from different jurors

- the nature of the interventions made, and

- the sources on which jurors were drawing to make their inputs

At the end of each jury I met briefly with jurors again to ask them to record their initial impressions and to arrange for follow up telephone interviews or questionnaires. Both before and after contacts with jurors were in the presence of facilitators.

Telephone interviews were conducted with jurors, witnesses and commissioners after the juries. Some jurors had expressed a preference to be sent questionnaires rather than be contacted by telephone and in a few cases where it was not possible to make contact by phone questionnaires were also sent. In all, ten telephone interviews were conducted with the Swansea jurors, nine with the Belfast jurors. Four questionnaires were returned by Swansea jurors and three by Belfast jurors. There were six jurors in total with whom it was not possible to make contact after the juries.

3. The jurors

The selection criteria underpinning juror recruitment required demographic profiling of both areas. In Belfast this was the area covered by the EHSSB, while in the case of the Swansea jury recruitment was from a single constituency – Swansea East. In Belfast 3,000 people were randomly selected from the Electoral Register and invited to take part in the jury by letter. At the same time as they received the invitation letter they were asked to complete a questionnaire collecting demographic information. Of the 251 who replied positively to the invitation 16 were selected to match the area profile on the basis of age, gender, social class and religion.

The ethnic composition of the population was such that a maximum of one black or Asian juror might have been included and this was considered to present the risk of tokenism.

Irf Swansea 16 young people were recruited to match the social class and gender profile of the area. Once again, the profile only included white people.

Questionnaires completed by the jurors at the start of the jury provided more information about those who agreed to take part. Because it was not possible to collect similar information about those who did not accept the invitation to take part, it is not possible to answer part of the first question posed in this evaluation: 'how do those who accept the invitation to participate differ from those who decline the invitation?' But it does enable us to say something about who did accept the invitation and their reasons for doing so. The intention in collecting this information was not to establish the 'representativeness' of the jurors in terms of the population from which they were drawn. Rather it was to understand more about the circumstances and motivations of those who responded positively to the invitation to take part in this experiment in participative democracy. This also makes it possible to consider both practical and substantive implications in terms of whose voices were and whose were not heard in the deliberative process. These implications are considered in Chapter 8.

The Belfast jurors

Of the nine men and seven women in the Belfast jury eight were married or living with a partner, five were single or living separately and one was widowed. In line with the recruitment profile they were all white. None reported having a physical or sensory impairment.

Table 3.1 Ages of Belfast jurors

Under 20	1
21-30	4
31-40	2
41-50	3
51-60	3
61-70	3

Among the occupations recorded by the Belfast jurors were: a teacher, a computer analyst, managers, a childminder, and a porter.

Table 3.2 Occupations of Belfast jurors

Working in full-time paid employment	7
Working in part-time paid employment	3
Full-time student	1
Part-time student	2
Main person responsible for care of home	2
Main person responsible for care of children	1
Main person responsible for care of other relatives/friends	0
Retired	4
Unemployed	1
Involved in voluntary work	1

The Swansea jurors

The Swansea jury involved 8 young women and 8 young men, aged 15-16. Once again they were all white. They all lived in two-generational households, all but one with siblings as well as one or more parents. None lived with grandparents, foster parents, or in a residential unit. None had visible impairments, but two reported having long-term illnesses: asthma and diabetes.

All but two reported that one or more parents were in paid work and half of these young people lived with parents who were involved in some type of public service work (including a policeman and a teacher). Seven of the jurors themselves had paid work. Four also had family responsibilities – in three cases this involved looking after younger siblings, in the fourth a dog. Interestingly the three who recorded responsibilities to look after younger siblings were all boys.

In view of the particular purpose of the MDA jury the young people were asked about their contact with older people. Most reported having regular contact with family members of their grandparents' generation via regular family visits or outings. Some also had contact with older people who are not family members within their neighbourhoods, through church, playing in a band, or contact with friends' relatives. However, it was evident that the jurors' interpretation of 'older people' included adults of all ages. This was a case of poor wording on the questionnaire by a middle-aged researcher!

Most of the jurors in both juries considered that those taking part represented a cross-section of people living in their areas. Only two of the Swansea jurors did not consider this to be the case, one of whom could not specify the sort of people he thought were not represented. The other was very definite in her view that the jurors did not represent a cross-section of young people in the area. She identified the absence of people from minority ethnic groups and considered that the number of jurors meant that insufficiently different views were represented among those taking part.

None of the Belfast jurors identified any absences in terms of the type of people represented on the jury, although one person expressed some uncertainty about this. He felt that it was only in the small group sessions that some people's views were heard so he was uncertain whether all 'community views' were represented. The meaning of the term 'a cross-section of people' may have a particular significance in Belfast in view of the religious separation of communities. This did not surface as an explicit issue in discussions, but it is possible that the use of the term 'community views' may have represented an uncertainty about the representation of views from both sections of the community in Belfast.[4]

Why take part?

By definition the jury model involves people who have been selected by various forms of random sampling. They have the option of declining the invitation to take part, but not to opt in. The jurors are not there because they have decided to respond to an open invitation (as is the case in public meetings), nor because they have actively sought out an opportunity to have their say. While participation in a jury is voluntary in the sense of not being 'coerced', participants are paid for their time. This is intended to minimise the likelihood that people will be excluded from taking part by losing out on employment income, but it may also affect motivation to participate. It is a characteristic of citizens' juries which distinguishes them from many other examples of user or public participation and a factor affecting their overall cost.

Table 3.3 Responses to the invitation to take part

	Swansea	Belfast
I was pleased to be invited	8	14
I wasn't sure what I would have to offer to the discussion	9	8
I was glad my ideas were being sought	10	8
I wondered what we were going to be discussing	11	10
I wasn't sure if I would be interested in the subject to be discussed	2	3
I would have liked to know what was to be discussed	4	5
I didn't really feel such an event would make a difference	1	0
I was worried about discussing with people I didn't know	4	3
I would have preferred to take part in such a discussion with people I know	6	0
I was concerned about the amount of time that would be involved	2	1
I was glad to be offered a fee to take part	9	9

Two Swansea responses were discounted because all boxes were ticked. However both the young men concerned responded to the open question about why they decided to come by saying they wanted the money. Thus we can confidently add two to the category 'I was glad to be offered a fee to take part' which was obviously a factor for over half those who accepted the invitation to become jurors.

So why did people decide to take part? If we look first at the young people who participated in the Swansea jury their reasons fall into the following categories:

● to have their say

● to ensure *young people*'s views were heard

- to hear other people's views

- because they were being paid to come

- general interest and curiosity

- to meet new people

- to have something to do

Eight identified money as one of their main reasons for accepting the invitation.

How do the reasons offered by the Belfast jurors for taking part compare with those identified by the young people in Swansea? Certain categories of responses were the same: there was curiosity about and interest in the idea, the fee was an important consideration for some jurors, and the opportunity to have their views heard was also significant. But some other reasons were also suggested:

- the jury was seen as an opportunity to broaden knowledge

- it was seen as something which might contribute to personal development and thus future opportunities

- some expressed a particular interest in making a contribution to health and health service issues

- there was some interest in what benefit a citizens' jury might be to the community at large.

There was more concern among the young people than among the adult jurors about taking part in this kind of deliberation with people they did not know. The young people had been recruited in pairs and some knew each other before the jury because they attended the same school. Five indicated that this had affected their decision to take part.

The Belfast jurors were less concerned about deliberating with strangers and, while two discovered they did know each other when they arrived, this had not affected their decisions to take part. While we do not know whether those not accepting the invitation to take part were inhibited by the prospect of engaging in discussion with strangers, there is at least some indication that the opportunity to engage with unknown others was viewed positively by those who took part as both a social and a developmental opportunity. This confirms experience in very different contexts in which people embrace the opportunity to have their say. [5]

Motivations also reflect the importance attached to the opportunity to have their say and to be part of a process which could make a positive contribution to the community. For the young people this was particularly significant because young people's voices are rarely heard in such contexts.

4. The process of deliberation

Deliberation is the basis on which the citizens' jury model is built. Evaluation must address the deliberative process directly if claims about the capacity to enable informed dialogue among citizens and between citizens and experts are to be assessed. Do the citizen participants become more informed, more able to engage in debate during the course of the jury process? Are all able to engage equally in this process?

In both juries deliberation took place in both plenary and small group sessions. In both cases the small group sessions were planned as opportunities for the jurors to engage in discussion among themselves, largely unfacilitated, and unobserved. This meant it was not possible to observe small group sessions for the purposes of the evaluation. However, such sessions were observed on the third day of the Belfast jury by which time the jurors felt sufficiently comfortable with each other and with the process not to be inhibited by the presence of the observer. Comments from the jurors indicated that they were largely unaware of the observer's presence during these discussions. It was clear from this limited observation of small groups sessions that the nature of the deliberative process was indeed different from that which took place within the plenary sessions (at least in some groups) and thus the detailed analysis of jury process which follows must be considered incomplete. Nevertheless, it was possible to observe and record the outcomes of the small group sessions when groups fed back in plenary.

Observations were designed to record who was contributing to the discussion, the nature of the input they were making and the sources on which they were drawing to make their input. This was intended to enable reflection on the extent to which the process was one in which all were able to engage equally, on the way in which jurors were able to engage with and use the information they were receiving from witnesses, on the way in which they drew from their own knowledge and experiences to contribute to the discussion, and on the extent of disagreement and the way in which this was dealt with during the course of debate. The input from facilitators was recorded in the same way as that of jurors. Sang and Davies (1998) provide a perspective on the citizens' jury process from the perspective of the facilitators. McIver's evaluation (1997) reflected on the different approaches to facilitation which can be adopted. My focus was on the overall deliberative process and the intention was to consider the part facilitators played in that process rather than focusing on the approach to facilitation per se.

The aim was to record each input during selected periods of the juries' deliberations. These periods were selected to encompass different types of sessions: they included periods when jurors were determining what questions they wanted to ask witnesses, periods when they were questioning witnesses, plenary discussions among jurors, and feedback from small group discussions. In practice, detailed recording was undertaken throughout most of the plenary sessions. While every effort was made to record each individual contribution there were times when this was difficult.

In order to report results relating to the process of deliberation while preserving the anonymity of jurors they were allocated pseudonyms.

The Belfast jury

The most obvious result of the analysis of the jurors' deliberations was the very different level of contribution from jurors in the plenary discussions.

Table 4.1 Belfast: Total numbers of contributions

Edna	130	David	57
Jane	129	Keith	45
Bill	123	Kenneth	42
Graham	101	Steven	40
Barry	99	Ann	7
Sally	87	Kate	5
Geraldine	84	Stewart	1
Sue	74	Debra	0

The precise number of interventions is not really the issue and no calculations (of 'average' input, for example) have been made on the basis of these. The intention is to demonstrate, on the basis of as comprehensive a recording as possible, differences in the extent to which jurors were actively engaged in the process of deliberation. It was evident both to facilitators and to the jurors themselves that there were some people who were playing very little part in the plenary discussion.

While the facilitator did from time to time encourage or invite contributions from those who were playing little part, observations suggested that it had been decided that the small group sessions would be more likely to provide an opportunity for participation by those who were obviously reluctant to speak in the full group. The limited observation of small groups indicated that while there were indeed some contributions from Ann, Kate, Stewart and Debra, their input was still considerably less in terms of quantity than others. There were three women in this 'low input' group, but the overall picture does not suggest that there was a particular gender difference in the level of contributions being made. Three of those who took little active part in plenary discussions were the three youngest members of the jury.

In order to illustrate the dynamics of the process of deliberation, and the extent and way in which jurors were drawing on information or evidence from their own experience and from that presented to them during the jury process, extracts of observation recordings will be presented in narrative form followed by a discussion of key aspects of the process.

Plenary feedback from small group discussions during which jurors had considered their responses to witnesses

The witnesses had been an officer of the Board, a fundholding GP and an independent commentator on the health service. The aim had been to enable jurors to understand the current organisation of the health service so that they knew the starting point for the proposed changes. It took place on the first day of the jury.

The facilitator asked jurors to feed back what they considered to be the positive aspects of the current situation. Graham, Bill and Kenneth reported the views of people in their groups. Jane commented that they had already discussed all of this and then Geraldine, Sue and Kenneth fed in other views about the current situation. Barry, referring back to the evidence of the witnesses, commented that they had found it difficult to make a judgement about many of the issues referred to because none of the jurors worked in this field, nor had financial experience or knowledge. Edna commented that she knew about this because she had worked in the health service and she compared her experience with that reported by the doctor witness. Jane referred back to a particular point made by the GP saying she didn't understand why he had to spend time on paper work when he had a manager. This led to a discussion involving Graham, Sue, Jane and Edna about the role of doctors in undertaking administrative tasks. There was a difference of view between Graham and Sue about this.

Keith referred back to a view previously expressed during the course of discussions and Graham commented on this. Keith suggested that the contribution of one of the witnesses they had just heard from meant their previous view was 'pie in the sky'. Edna referred to evidence from one of the witnesses about the proportion of the budget spent on management costs to make a comment on this. The facilitator summed up the previous discussion suggesting that they had highlighted a key point and Bill and Jane responded with views about this. The facilitator then asked if anyone had anything to add at this point. This led to an extended discussion of GP fundholding during which jurors were referring to witness evidence. Sally suggested they should be cautious about accepting his view: 'he would say that wouldn't he', while Keith said he would believe the doctor. Sally then referred to the experience of a friend of hers being told by her doctor to buy her medication. The facilitator asked jurors what they considered the key issue was in relation to this and suggested it might be an issue to do with consistency of behaviour. Sally disagreed suggesting it was a question of funding. Bill suggested it was about budgetary control.

During the previous session in which jurors had heard from witnesses, most of the questions and exchanges had been with the GP rather than the other two witnesses. There had been only one question to the independent analyst. This, together with jurors' concerns about their lack of expert knowledge on issues of finance meant that much of the discussion focused around the GP's input. Virtually all citizens have either personal experience of GPs or can draw on family members' experiences and this is likely to make discussion in this area more comfortable, including the possibility of questioning the objectivity of views expressed. Another feature of this session was the early indication that jurors' 'uninformed' assessments of priorities might be changed as a result of information presented by witnesses. Witness evidence was not accepted uncritically and personal experience was used to suggest alternative perspectives.

An exchange between jurors and a witness

The witness was an officer of the EHSSC who had presented evidence about the role of the Council in representing the views of the public to the Board. She had talked about a variety of methods by which they might do this and had discussed the situation relating to public participation in Board meetings. The context was a session in which jurors were being invited to focus on the issue of public participation in health service decision making. It took place on the third day of the jury.

At the end of her evidence Bill started with a challenging comment about the capacity of the Council to speak on behalf of people when no-one has ever heard of them. He also interpreted a comment about interviewing potential Council members as 'vetting' and asked a challenging question about that. The witness clarified the interview process and Bill apologised.

Geraldine commented to the witness on the uselessness of making Board meetings more accessible suggesting that decisions have been made before the meeting starts. The witness responded from her experience of such meetings. Jane then asked a factual question: 'Does a representative of the Council always attend a Board meeting?' The witness responded with a clarification of Board procedure. Bill then expressed the view that the system should be changed and Barry also suggested that it is an exercise in public relations.

Edna (who used to work in the health service) referred to ex-colleagues' experience of Board meetings and suggested it is very difficult for people to stand up and speak in this context. The witness responded to this.

There was then an exchange between Bill, Edna and Geraldine who suggested that the public should be able to go and speak directly at Board meetings. The process then moved on to the next witness.

This exchange demonstrated that jurors were prepared to be quite challenging to witnesses. The witness was prepared to respond to those challenges, but her input suggested that she was trying not to lead jurors, but to respond specifically to the questions they asked. She appeared to reflect on this, and asked to come back later in the session in order to explain in more detail ways in which the Board listened to representations from the Council. She was concerned that since the questions had focused only on opportunities for people to speak at Board meetings that the jurors had been left with an unbalanced impression of the role and activities of the Council.

Plenary session during which jurors were pulling together their deliberations to produce the report with their recommendations

The facilitator started by summing up what jurors had previously identified as 'good things' about the health service and invited jurors to suggest any changes to this or whether there are any disagreements to the issues previously identified. Sally and Ann suggested a qualification to one of the previous points based on further deliberations that had taken place. Sally referred to the input of a GP witness in this respect. The jurors made no further amendment to the characteristics they had previous identified as 'good'.

The facilitator invited them to suggest any amendments to the characteristics previously identified as 'bad'. Edna suggested that one of the points they had made previously was 'not a headline issue'. Sue, who had been the one who had identified this point based on personal experiences of family members, disagreed. Graham and Sally expressed differing views on this, then Edna suggested that it might be expressed differently. Barry made another suggestion referring back to the evidence from a witness the jurors themselves had requested (someone who could speak from experience of using health and social services – in this case the mother of a son with learning difficulties). Sue commented on this referring back to her original idea about this point. Edna and Bill expressed their views on the matter and Sally made a comment based on the GP's input. Edna and Bill made further comments. The facilitator then intervened to ask what was the particular issue that was emerging from this discussion. Edna and Sue expressed their views about this, then Graham suggested that there were in fact two issues involved in what they were discussing. Geraldine, Sue, Graham, Sally and Kenneth made further comments and the issue was resolved by agreeing to change the way in which the point had been worded.

The discussion continued in a similar vein with a view to finalising the jurors' recommendations.

During this process the jurors were drawing on a range of witness inputs to refine their original criteria for a 'good' health service. Some differences of emphasis and perspective emerged at this stage, with an attempt to distinguish issues which may have been merged earlier in the debate as a means of seeking to resolve difference. The facilitator was playing a more active role than at some stages in seeking to draw out key points from the jurors' discussion. A similar role was also being played by one of the jurors. There was some sense of urgency in completing the task in time to make the report at the end of the jury and this appeared to push jurors to find ways of accommodating difference rather than engaging with it.

The following characteristics of the process of deliberation are revealed from a review of these and other observation recordings:

- The jurors were not only making use of witness evidence but also drawing on their own or others' experiences to contribute to the discussion. This may be one factor contributing to unequal input from jurors throughout the jury. Younger jurors with less life experience may feel they have less to contribute.

- There were differences in the extent to which jurors 'believed' what witnesses told them, or were prepared to accept this as an unbiased reflection of reality. Some degree of familiarity may give jurors greater confidence to question the views expressed by witnesses – either to their face or in discussion among themselves afterwards.

- In addition to variation in credibility, witnesses were regarded as having varying degrees of usefulness. Neither the independent analyst nor the academic witness called to provide broader views on health service developments and developing models of public participation were regarded as particularly useful. After the latter had left, jurors were critical about the inaccessible language he had used in giving evidence.

- The jurors' behaviour towards witnesses was always polite, even when they appeared to be gaining little positive input from the witnesses (indicated by few follow up questions, or questions which led to little follow-up discussion). They differed noticeably in their response to different witnesses. For example, the mother of a disabled child was called as a witness as a result of a request from jurors themselves. The initial response to her was an expression of congratulation for her action on her own behalf and on behalf of others in a similar position. The overall interaction with this witness appeared much more relaxed and was characterised by an easy and extended exchange involving eight of the 16 jurors. This contrasts with the exchanges between jurors and an officer of the Board earlier in the jury which involved only two jurors putting one question each.

- There was considerable debate among the jurors themselves, with the facilitator intervening primarily to summarise, clarify or move the discussion on, rather than to lead or even prompt discussion. Certain of the jurors at different stages adopted similar roles to that of the facilitator in summarising or highlighting the issues emerging from discussions.

● The jurors engaged with complex, detailed issues in response to witness evidence. However, there were times when this appeared to be at the expense of engaging with the bigger picture. The witnesses jurors found most difficult to engage with were those who offered a more strategic view. Those talking about particular circumstances or experiences were often closely questioned on this.

● Differences of view were expressed by different jurors and a resolution was sometimes offered by another juror not directly involved in the particular discussion. There was some evidence that this was a role played by two or three of the jurors. The facilitator asked questions intended to clarify points of difference. She did not seek directly to suggest how differences might be resolved.

The Swansea jury

Turning to the deliberations of the Swansea jury we can again see a considerable range in the level of input to plenary discussions by different jurors.

Table 4.2 Swansea: Total numbers of contributions

Liz	53	Michael	9
Ruth	53	Luke	6
Iona	31	Jeffrey	5
Guy	30	Carys	4
Jan	27	Gwyn	3
Tina	24	Helen	2
Ben	17	Peter	2
John	10	Cathy	1

Once again the actual numbers are less significant than the distribution. But one fact which is evident from this is the comparative level of input from the young women in comparison with the young men – five of the six making the most frequent interventions were young women. The decision that group sessions when young people were working together should not be observed meant that it was not possible to consider the nature of deliberation amongst young people when they were in a much stronger position to determine the rules of the game. During groupwork sessions different means of deliberation were used – including visual techniques such as designing urban environments. It is likely that the exchanges which took place during such exercises were different from those observed in the plenary sessions.

If we look more closely at the nature of the interventions being made in plenary and at the nature of the interactive process involved we also see considerable differences from the deliberative process in the Belfast jury described above. Once again, descriptive narratives from the process recording can be used to illustrate examples of the deliberative process.

Plenary discussion to review and develop previously produced lists of likes and dislikes about their neighbourhoods

This was the first substantive session of the jury. Previously there had been a warm-up and a ground-rule setting session.

> The facilitator introduced the task. Different lists had been produced by different groups during a preliminary meeting of the jurors and the facilitator invited those involved in producing the first list to reflect and comment on it. Liz provided an initial response. The facilitator then asked all the jurors a questions about this. Guy and Michael responded. The facilitator then asked another question. Jan responded. The facilitator asked another question about the list. There were non-verbal responses from the jurors. The facilitator asked three more questions before she received a response from Liz. The facilitator then asked the group producing the list a question and Liz responded. The facilitator then asked Liz a question and she responded to the facilitator. The facilitator put a question to all the jurors and Ruth responded. The facilitator then responded directly to Ruth. The process continued in this question – response mode between facilitator and jurors.

Witness session – the witnesses were an environmental campaigner, a policeman and a housing association officer
This took place on the afternoon of the first full day of the jury.

Following presentations from three witnesses one after the other, the jurors were asked to break into three groups and to come up with at least two questions to put to the witnesses. Before they broke into groups there was some discussion about what sort of questions they might ask and John asked the facilitator if she would ask a question. She said she would not. There was an exchange between Ruth, John, Michael and Guy about a particular question that they wanted to put to one of the witnesses.

When the witnesses came back in Liz was the first to put a question. This was to the environmental campaigner and concerned ways in which people could be encouraged to cycle and walk rather than use cars. He responded with examples. Ruth then asked a similar question. The witness responded with examples.

The facilitator then invited other jurors to put a question. Michael asked a question of the same witness: 'Is yours a well-paid job?' The witness responded. Jan then asked the same witness a question about the nature of his job and he responded. Ruth then expressed a view to the witness about the benefits of cars. Liz disagreed with Ruth about this. The witness responded. The facilitator then invited other jurors to put questions. Iona, Ruth, Jan and Ben then put questions to the housing association officer who responded. The questions from jurors at this point flowed on from those previously put and Ben's question referred back to something the policeman witness had said. It was not clear whether these were the questions which jurors had previously decided to put, or whether they were prompted by the exchanges that were developing.

The facilitator invited other questions and Iona put a question to the policeman. He responded and Iona made a comment in response to his reply. The witness agreed with her comment and expanded on this. Michael then put the question which had been the subject of discussion among jurors when they were preparing. He asked the policeman if he had ever taken drugs. The policemen replied and Michael followed up with another question making two further inputs. Ruth then put another question and the policeman responded to her. Michael then told a story of his experience and the witness responded to this. The facilitator invited further questions. There were none and the session closed.

Feedback from groupwork

This session took place on the morning of the second full day of the jury. The jurors had been working on coming up with headlines about issues young people think are important to take into account when planning neighbourhoods.

Tina was the first to feed back from her group. She described the issues they had come up with and the reasons for them. Jan then provided feedback from her group. They had taken up the suggestion that this should be in the form of a newspaper article and this drew on the collective experience of young people. Ben then fed back from his group.

The facilitators then put flip charts with groupwork on the walls and invited the jurors to look at and comment the points being made. Gwyn identified what he saw as one of the key messages coming from these. Other jurors expressed their agreement. One of the facilitators then invited other comments. Iona, Michael, John and Liz made suggestions. The facilitator sought the views of jurors about these. Iona expressed a view. The facilitator invited other responses. Jeffrey made a suggestion. There was then some exchange between jurors with some disagreement about whether

Swansea had better shops for boys or girls. The facilitator then invited any other suggestions: 'it's your last chance'. Guy made a comment 'I bet nothing happens about all this'. The facilitator then pointed out that they had six suggestions and the intention had been to have five – could they select. Ruth made a comment and Tina disagreed. There was then an exchange involving Iona, Liz and a number of others which became quite lively and drew on some personal experiences. Guy and John had a disagreement about the use of CCTV. There were then a series of exchanges among the young people about drug taking and whether this should be legalised. The facilitator called them back to focus on the issues they had listed on flip charts. The observers' notes at this point read: 'There is laughter and calling out. Some people are trying to make serious points in the middle of all this. A level of excitement has set in. People are calling out ideas, suggestions, agreement, disagreement. The facilitator tries to get them focused on the flip chart. When she insists they go quiet.'

These examples, which are typical of the jury as a whole, illustrate a number of points about the process of the Swansea jury:

- Many of the exchanges were question and answer exchanges between jurors and facilitators or between jurors and witnesses.

- Exchanges between the jurors themselves in plenary sessions were rather limited. When they did take place they were characterised by quick-fire, bantering-type interactions where people were talking on top of each other.

- The issue which caused interest and excitement among the young people was that of drug taking. Since this was not one which was seen to relate directly to the jury 'charge' the jurors deliberations on this topic were not encouraged.

- It was evident that the young people were drawing on personal experiences to some extent, although overall there was less specific reference to personal experiences as a source of ideas than there was in Belfast. There was also comparatively little direct reference to witness evidence or to other sources of information being drawn on in the process of deliberation.

Jurors' responses to the process

The jurors' overall responses to the jury and some of the specific questions posed in post jury interviews allow further reflection on the process of deliberation which developed in these two citizens' juries.

The immediate responses of jurors to the experience were mainly positive ones. From both sets of jurors there was a sense that it had been a worthwhile experience, although the degree of active enjoyment varied. For example, the following responses from Swansea jurors reflect different experiences:

I didn't not like it, but I didn't really enjoy it extremely.

When I first came in I didn't know what it was about but then I thought it was all right – it was something for me to do. I liked taking part it was good fun.

The Belfast jurors more consistently rated the experience as not only worthwhile, but one which they had got something out of. For example:

I was very impressed and derived a good degree of satisfaction and a fair degree of knowledge from taking part in the exercise.

I found the jury very interesting and informative and gave me experience in discussion and gave me a chance to meet new people from different backgrounds.

If we look at the 'good things' and 'not so good things' cited by jurors immediately after the juries we get more insight into their overall responses. For the young people the jury provided an opportunity to have their views heard, to hear the views of others and to discuss with them, to meet other young people with whom most thought they got on well, and to earn £75. These were all cited positively. When asked to identify one not so good thing, nine young people thought the process went on too long, three thought the tasks they were asked to undertake were repetitive or boring and one thought some people had not had sufficient opportunity to contribute to discussions. The other less positive aspect of the event which was cited was the poor quality of the food.

The Belfast jurors were more likely to cite aspects of the deliberative process when asked to identify one good thing about the jury. Examples of this included:

Operated along democratic lines.

Good interaction in the group.

Challenged your preconceptions.

It gave everyone involved an adequate opportunity to put forward his/her opinion and discuss all ideas generally.

There was also reference to the jury as a source of specific information and learning about health and social services, as well as being an opportunity to 'have your say'.

In contrast with the Swansea jurors, the one thing which Belfast jurors identified as 'not so good' was insufficient time adequately to get to grips with and resolve views about the issues under discussion. The following comments reflect this:

Perhaps endeavouring too much too quickly.

At the beginning we did not get enough time to question witnesses – other questions we asked relating to Board and other respective activities – we were not able to get immediate answers to questions asked – ie observers perhaps could have answered questions asked.

Not enough information prior to the jury.

Sometimes the issues were difficult to come to a decided agreement on and some of the issues were over-complicated.

However, six jurors said they could not identify anything when asked to record one 'not so good thing' about the jury.

In the follow up interviews a number of comments were made by Belfast jurors about the process of deliberation:

- There was a sense that jurors were genuinely enabled to express their own views.

- Representatives from the Board who were at the jury were seen to be genuine in their wish to hear from the general public.

- The nature of the interaction between jurors was experienced positively. Not only the jurors but some witnesses and observers spoke of how quickly the jury seemed to gel.

- There were some comments about the quality of the input from other jurors

Specific interview questions were asked about disagreement and difference within the deliberative process. These were prompted, in part, by jurors themselves identifying the way in which difference was dealt with as one criterion to be used in assessing the extent to which the jury would have been worthwhile.

In the Belfast jury six jurors said they found themselves in agreement with other jurors most of the time. Others made a variety of qualifying statements about the level of agreement they experienced. For example, one, who estimated that he felt in agreement about 70 per cent of the time identified one specific issue on which he had not found himself in agreement with others, but said that his view on this had shifted during the deliberations. Another suggested that there were times when people were expressing personal views based on personal experiences and this was the source of some difference of view. Three felt that their different views did not come across adequately in the final report. The others felt that the report encompassed the range of views expressed or represented a consensus. There was broad agreement that the process as a whole had enabled different views to be explored, although there were also some qualifying comments about this. The time issue was referred to as acting to limit the full exploration of the range of different issues raised. One person suggested that they had been able to 'engage with disagreement' – to agree to disagree – as well as to resolve differences.

Another commented on the skill of the moderator in getting people engaged and expressed confidence that if there had been disagreement she would have drawn these out. This person felt the deliberations had largely been characterised by consensus. A rather different interpretation is suggested by another comment 'Different views were touched on. However the fact that the majority tended to be of the same opinion on most issues perhaps had the effect of concentrating on one area at the peril of another'. A rather similar view was suggested by someone who felt that the time pressures involved in producing a report by a deadline meant they were always scratching at the surface of issues and that if more in-depth discussion had taken place more disagreement might have been revealed.

The jurors were largely satisfied with the range of witnesses they heard from, including those they had requested themselves. Some would have liked more time with some of the witnesses and it was also suggested that some of the observers could have answered questions raised by jurors but they were not allowed to. The following possible additions were suggested: a hospital doctor or clinical manager in a hospital, more of the 'high up ones...these guys on £160,000 per year', 'maybe more at the bottom end like carers... I have a couple of daughters who are carers...they didn't have a say'. The usefulness of some of the witnesses who *were* there was also questioned.

The overall responses of Swansea jurors also made reference to issues of process. In addition to general points about the opportunity it offered to express opinions and to discuss issues, there were the following comments:

'I liked the way it was done, but not the hours. I would have liked more time on the first two days, less on the last two.'

'The exercises were good – a good variety.'

'It was good because we got to a couple of decisions.'

'It was relaxed and friendly.'

'You had to do more thinking as well as give your opinions.'

'It was fun to do.'

Eight Swansea jurors felt they had been in agreement with other jurors most of the time. One who said she had not been in agreement noted that the small groups enabled everyone's opinion to be given and that some of that came over at the end in the production of the final report. But she also suggested that people did not change their views during the course of deliberation. Only one person felt that his different views did not come over in the final report.

Since the young people's jury was shorter than typical adult juries there was no opportunity for the young people to identify witnesses they themselves would have liked to hear from. When asked if there were other people they might have wanted to invite to be witnesses three people made suggestions: other people involved in city planning, particularly those who might be involved in bringing activities into the city, a greater variety of people, including people from outside Swansea because that would have brought in ideas from people who know what things are like elsewhere, and shop owners (particularly clothes and shoe shop owners).

5. Building citizenship?

One of the questions posed in this evaluation was whether involvement in a citizens' jury has any impact on people's sense of themselves as citizens. Some of the questions asked of jurors by means of the questionnaires completed before the jury took place were designed to explore the extent to which jurors were already engaged in activities which could be understood as constituting 'active citizenship' within the public sphere. The possibilities to express the formal status of citizenship are different for adults than they are for 15-16 year olds and thus this part of the questionnaire differed for the two groups.

The Swansea jurors

Two said they had written to their MP and two to their local councillor. None had contacted their MEP. None said they had attended a local council meeting, attended a Parliamentary debate or lobbied a member of Parliament.

Two young people ticked all the 'have been a member' boxes in relation to all the organisation boxes. One ticked all but one of the 'have been' boxes and one 'currently' box. I am not confident that these are accurate responses. Apart from these, five were currently members of sports or leisure organisations and three had been members of such organisations. One was currently a member of a youth organisation and three had been in the past. One was currently a member of a religious organisation. One had been a member of a school council, and one had been a member of both a voluntary organisation and a self help group.

In addition ten had signed a petition, two had attended a public meeting and three had taken part in a demonstration.

The Belfast jurors

Most were regular voters in elections. Only one had written to a local councillor and none to an MP or MEP. Similarly only one had attended a council meeting and none had attended a Parliamentary debate or lobbied a Member of Parliament.

Table 5.1 Voting habits of Belfast jurors

	Never	Sometimes	Usually	Always
Local elections	1	2	5	8
National elections	0	1	5	7
European elections	2	2	1	7

Few were currently members of the type of voluntary associations indicative of an active civil society, but more indicated that they had at some stage of their lives been members of such associations:

Table 5.2 Voluntary association membership

	Current	Former
Political party	0	2
Trades union	1	4
Professional association	1	4
Voluntary organisations	1	3
Campaigning group	0	0
Self-help group	0	1
Religious organisation	2	4
Sports or leisure organisation	3	6

None had held unpaid public office. However half had previously attended a public meeting and 14 of the 16 had signed a petition at some stage in their lives.

Table 5.3 Political action

Signed a petition	14
Attended a public meeting	8
Gone on strike	5
Taken part in a demonstration	3
Taken part in direct action	4

Assessing the impact of an intense but brief experience as a member of a citizens' jury on people's sense of themselves as citizens, and on what might be considered their practice as citizens, can only start to suggest the way in which such involvement might build citizenship.

Jurors' responses to questions intended to capture some sense of the impact the jury had had on them were as follows:

Table 5.4 Numbers taking action since the jury

	Swansea	Belfast
Discussed what happened at the jury with someone who was at the jury	7	8
Discussed what happened at the jury with someone who was not at the jury	12	12
Read anything about any of the topics that were discussed at the jury	2	8
Watched a TV programme about any of the topics that were discussed at the jury	2	7
Been in touch with any organisation involved in some way with the issues discussed at the jury	0	1
Anything else prompted by your experience of the jury	0	5

One reason for the difference in follow-up between the two juries may be because of differences in opportunities. The Belfast jurors collected written material from witnesses, from the jury commissioners and facilitators and thus took away with them material for follow up reading. It is also possible that there were more TV programmes dealing with issues to do with the health service than about the built environment which was the focus for the Swansea jury. The Belfast jurors were also invited to attend both the Board meeting at which their report was discussed and a special meeting of the EHSSC. One of the Swansea jurors reported reading an item in the local paper about planning issues and another reported watching a Channel 4 youth programme *Wise Up* which had focused on ways in which people might help their local council.

Most had conversations with families and/or friends about the jury itself and the topics which were the subject of deliberation. Some Belfast jurors had deliberately sought conversations with people they knew who worked in the health service to pursue issues raised during the jury. There was thus a sense of 'spreading the word' and the potential for the impact of the jury to extend beyond the direct participants. There was evidence of jurors having some continuing contact with each other in the period immediately after the juries. Indeed, I was able to undertake two interviews with Swansea jurors during one phone call because two who had become friends as a result of taking part in the jury were together when I called. Some of the Belfast jurors reported an increase in knowledge about health service issues which was of relevance in the context of their own or a family members' use of health services.

The concept of 'citizen' promoted by advocates of deliberative democracy is someone who is able to engage in informed deliberation on issues of public policy. Most of the jurors thought they had learned from being involved in the jury and thus might be considered to have greater potential to act in this way in future as a result.

Table 5.5 Number reporting learning from the jury process

	Swansea	Belfast
From the contributions of witnesses	10	12
From other jurors	12	12
From the experience of being involved in this sort of discussion – expressing your views and hearing the different views of other people	10	9

The type of learning which jurors identified can be categorised as follows:

● New information

how people plan the city (S)

the difference between fundholders and non-fundholders (B)

the existence of the health and social services council (B)

● Increased understanding

about the way other people live, what different areas are like (S)

the reasons why people do what they do (S)

an insight into the role these people played in the NHS and how the working of the NHS affects them (B)

referring to the contributions of witnesses:

they had very personalised overviews of what they are involved in.

Their personal views help you to understand because they are not detached (B)

- Awareness of different views and experiences

We all want different things – some want all-night clubs, others smaller clubs (S)

Other people's views are different from mine (S)

Other jurors gave different points of view that I hadn't come across before (B)

Where I live in Belfast on the outskirts there is no problem …problems like hospitals closing…other jurors in those areas have experienced problems, I could empathise (B)

Other jurors did not know much (B)

- Encouraging reflection?

Everyone has their own opinion and you can't change them (S)

The main thing is people tend to think they're right. You hear views, get persuaded, see others' points of view because in an interactive situation you can adopt part of that view (B)

A lot of issues would never have crossed my mind. I got another look at the way people think about things (B)

A couple of things I was challenged on – it stopped you from being blinkered. You thought about things more (B)

- The deliberative process

How to present myself (S)

In the little rooms [small group sessions] we had to get things going in a focused direction. I did learn from that. I got more skills out of that (B)

I got the feeling that the agenda was leading us down a particular line (B)

The small groups gave us a chance to have a yarn and talk it over. Not as embarrassing to talk in small groups A lot didn't want to talk in the big group (B)

● The potential to achieve change

> *That something should be done by young people to make Swansea etc better* (S)

Most were sufficiently positive about the experience to say that they would take part in a citizens' jury again if asked. Eleven of the Swansea jurors said they would do so, seven of whom said they would take part if there was no payment. One said he would definitely not take part again because he had found it boring. Two said 'maybe', but would not take part if there was no payment.

Ten Belfast jurors said they would take part again – one of whom said he would be 'dying to' and seven who said unconditionally that they would do it if they were not paid. Two others offered conditional responses to the possibility of future participation: one who was concerned about the amount of time involved and suggested that she would take part if it ran for a couple of evenings rather than four days, the other suggested he would if he had the time and money.

The concept of citizenship is not one which is often part of everyday discourse. Yet the jurors had all agreed to take part in what was described to them as a 'citizens' jury'. So what did this term mean to them and how did they understand it in relation to themselves?

Many found it hard to define what the term meant, although most of those who offered a definition expressed an inclusive perspective on the meaning of citizenship. The young people used terms such as 'anyone', 'all people in the community', 'any person living in any area'. Some related it to concepts such as community, city or civilisation: 'a person who's part of the community', 'people within a civilisation', while one qualified the inclusiveness of the term: 'somebody in the community and wants the best for it'.

There were similar distinctions in the responses of the Belfast jurors between those who offered an unqualified definition: 'a member of the relevant community. Anyone in the community', 'someone who lives in and takes part in the community in the UK in whatever shape or form. It doesn't have to be an active participant, for example, Mr X may pay more taxes than Mr Y, but his view is not worth more', ' I took it as an ordinary person on the street. Could be anybody – top to bottom', and those who may have been influenced by their experience of the jury to suggest that 'being a citizen' might involve some active expression or 'practice' of citizenship: 'a part of the public. A representative of the public, interested in being a good citizen, someone willing to go on this jury', 'a "citizen" means a participant in social issues concerning that person'.

One thing that is evident from these responses is the absence of notions of 'citizenship rights' which have been the subject of considerable academic analysis and contestation in the context of concepts of citizenship. The only rights which were evident in these responses were the rights of 'ordinary people' or 'Joe Bloggs' to have their say about issues of public interest.

When the issue was put to them, jurors did not distance themselves from ideas of being 'a citizen', but it was clearly not a term that was central to their sense of themselves. Interestingly two jurors referred to their employment or class status in response to the question about whether they would describe themselves in this way (in the terms they had used to define what 'citizen' meant to them), while another suggested that she had been a citizen since she had retired. This may reflect the fact that 'senior citizen' is one of the few terms in general usage which incorporates the concept, but may also refer back to her response to what the term meant to her. She suggested that a 'citizen' was a member of the public and that if the intention had been to get together a cross section of the public then the jury organisers had been successful. But she also suggested that the jury would have been more effective if it had been composed of people with, as she put it 'more clout', such as business people, people who would be prepared to stand up and give their opinion to anyone, to carry on pursuing the issues outside the jury.

5. The 'experts'

Processes of deliberation and dialogue involve two-way exchanges. In addition to considering the impact of this on the 'ordinary citizens' invited to take part we also need to know whether this has any impact on the 'experts' called to give evidence and be questioned. The questions posed by the evaluation in this context were: Do they feel threatened or stimulated by being questioned? Do they learn from the process as well as contributing to the learning of the citizens involved? Do they become more open to engaging with citizens in decision making as a result of this experience? Does such involvement enhance their own sense of citizenship?

The final question highlights an issue which has already been touched on. While the terms 'professional' or 'expert' set apart those trained and educated to acquire specialist knowledge from 'ordinary citizens', the definition of 'citizen' is intended to be an inclusive one – experts are citizens too. At the same time, one of the purposes of deliberative methods of participation is to draw on the 'ordinary knowledge' of 'ordinary citizens' and to validate this as a legitimate resource in decision making. In considering the impact of being involved in citizens' juries on witnesses we are thus considering the effect of different dynamics:

the experience of having professional knowledge or expertise challenged by reference to lay knowledge

the potential for learning from citizens as well as helping citizens learn, and

the potential for the process to build any sense of citizen solidarity between witnesses and jurors.

Such issues are complex and this study can only start to address them.

The Swansea witnesses

There were four witnesses to the Swansea jury: a police inspector working as a youth liaison officer, a director of a local authority planning department, the assistant director of a housing association and

a man working for an independent environmental agency. All wer
white and male.

Three of the four had previous experience of public consultation i
the course of their work, although none had been involved as a 'citizen'
Two said they had substantial contact with members of the public in th
course of doing their jobs, although none had frequent contact wit
young people. One had heard the term 'citizens' jury', but none had an
previous knowledge of this method of public involvement. All wer
positive about the idea when it was introduced to them, althougl
expressed some apprehension about their own involvement.

None of the witnesses did substantial preparation in advance of th
jury and two indicated that this was deliberate. They were concerne
that if they over prepared their input would be too complex. One use
the phrase 'from the hip' to describe how he thought he should mak
his input. The witnesses were aware of and somewhat wary abou
presenting information in a way which would be accessible to youn
people. But they also recognised that this was a worthwhile exercis
and were prepared to respond to the challenge.

Only one of the witnesses found himself personally challenged b
the young people's questions and this was a challenge that he wa
expecting. The policeman was asked whether he had ever taken drugs
During interview he said he had been waiting for the 'low ball' and i
came early on. He felt his truthful response created a positive respons
among the jurors. Witnesses used the words 'refreshing', 'stimulating
and 'relaxed' to describe the experience of presenting and bein
questioned, although one witness also observed smirks from som
jurors and was aware that some were losing interest.

Witnesses were somewhat reluctant to judge whether the jurors ha
learnt anything from their contributions. Only one identified a specifi
issue which had been a focus for jurors' questions (relating t
homelessness: how people become homeless and what the responsibility c
housing agencies is to this) which he had found surprising and about whicl
he thought some specific learning may have taken place on the part of th
young people. Another commented on the way in which the 'disciplined
approach to structuring the discussion had forced the young people t
concentrate on issues which they might otherwise not have considered.

Nor was there much of a sense that the witnesses had learnt from th
jurors. For example, one felt that the jurors were inhibited in thei

uestioning and that although there was an attempt to be informal the tmosphere was stressful, whilst another expressed himself disappointed y the jurors' views about older people.

Whilst all four witnesses felt positive enough about the experience to ay that they would do it again if asked, there was little sense that being witness at this jury had had a major impact on them, or that it was kely to have any significant effect on the way in which they might go bout their jobs in future. One suggested that there would need to be a eries of sessions like this before any real impact would be felt.

Their reactions to the concept of the 'citizen' reflected the nfamiliarity of the term within ordinary discourse in Great Britain.)ne described it as an 'old-fashioned' term that tended not to be used 1 relation to young people and that it didn't really capture what the jury vas intended to be all about. Another, who had a generally more ositive response to the whole experience suggested that as young eople tended to be excluded it was useful to apply the term specifically o work with young people. He went on to suggest that it should be ompulsory to have youth forums which would have a say in ommunity life. Another also reflected a more positive response to the oncept with which he identified. He described a citizen as 'someone vho is involved in your community and interested in decision-making rocesses'.

Overall, the sense from these witness responses was of a rather low ey experience which was not of itself capable of generating significant earning for either jurors or witnesses. There were differences in their esponses which reflected potential tensions in objectives of 'officials' eeking to engage the public. One view of this is that this is an pportunity to 'educate' the public about the responsibilities and mitation of public authorities. Another is that the main learning should e the other way – that public officials need to learn from those whose iews are rarely heard in decision-making circles. This jury was seen to ave had only limited success in achieving either objective.

he Belfast witnesses

nterviews were conducted with four of the witnesses to the Belfast jury nd questionnaires were returned by four others. Witnesses included fficers of the Eastern Health and Social Services Board, a GP, an officer

of the Eastern Health and Social Services Council, a communit
development for health worker, a volunteer with a disabilit
organisation and an academic working in the area of public consultatio
and community development.

All but one said they had previous experience of public consultatio
in their professional roles and two also had experience in their role a
'citizen'. One was also a parent governor. Collectively their experienc
included a range of methods of consultation and/or involvement: publi
meetings, surveys, focus groups, community development, patien
participation groups and consumer panels. All might therefore b
described as 'interested' in public participation and all expressed a
interest in the idea of citizens' juries. Some had specific questions abou
the method: whether it was capable of providing a truly 'representative
view, and whether the complexity of the topic was appropriate to th
method. Others saw in it the potential for overcoming some of th
limitations or dilemmas they had experienced in other methods: i
particular the issue of whether the views of knowledgeable activist
could be accepted as representative of less informed members of th
general public and as a means of moving from an oppositional to
more constructive process.

There was a difference of view about the appropriateness of th
particular topic for a citizens' jury. Those who questioned this referre
to the potential for media coverage to bias views about health services
the wide ranging issues contained within the consultation paper an
thus the complexity of the task involved, and the different level o
interest and knowledge of health and social services issues which migh
skew the content of discussions.

The responses of witnesses to the invitation to act in this role range
from 'I jumped at the chance' to 'terrified – extremely anxious'. Th
latter response came from a doctor who noted that being a witness wa
extremely threatening for a doctor. However, there was no indication o
this response from another doctor who also acted as a witness. Anothe
respondent spoke of the challenge of being appropriately informativ
without speaking down to people. Most did some preparation. Ther
was variation in the extent to which witnesses considered that they ha
prepared or presented material in ways which were different from th
approaches they might usually adopt. One said he was used to speakin
about complex issues to 'ordinary' members of the public, and anothe

that she found herself drawing on her own personal experiences of using the health service as much as on the knowledge that she had gained through working on health issues. However another suggested that the process of presenting material was very different from the way in which he usually went about this – 'behaving as normal was not an option' – and another referred to repeatedly scanning the material he had prepared to cut out technical jargon. Another noted that he had tried to cut out technical terms but received feedback which indicated to him that he had failed to achieve this.

There were a number of dimensions to the witnesses' experiences of presenting the material and being questioned on it:

- anxiety: the terms 'frightened', 'unsure', 'nerve wracking' were used as well as 'tension' and 'strain'

- general enjoyment and interest

- the degree of concentration required in order to think about issues being raised as well as communicating the key messages

- difficulties of getting over sufficient information in a short period of time

- enjoyment of the process of engaging with the jurors

- surprise and interest in particular attitudes being expressed

As in the Swansea jury, there was some uncertainty about whether the jury process had been a learning one for either jurors or witnesses. One witness compared the experience of being a witness at the jury with other experiences of public meetings. Her response is worth considering in some detail as it runs counter to some other views about the comparative opportunities for dialogue offered by public meetings and citizens' juries. She expressed disappointment at the lack of opportunity for interaction with the jury. She described giving her evidence, being asked questions by only a couple of jurors and then having no further involvement in the process. She said she had no sense of why the particular questions had been asked, nor whether they reflected broadly held views among jurors. While she was able to answer the questions put to her, this did not lead to any dialogue with the jurors who conducted a lot of their deliberations in private. In contrast, she suggested that while public meetings may be characterised by angry people coming with views to express, she felt she understood more about what those views were and why they were held, and more able to provide a helpful response by providing answers and engaging in an exchange about these than she had done in the jury. While this was a one-off response, there is some supporting evidence from the analysis of interactions which indicates that in some cases there was little dialogue between jurors and witnesses, and other witnesses (and jurors) reflected that the time available to engage with some topics was insufficient. Lack of time was cited by witnesses as limitation on what they thought could be learned from the interactions in which they were involved.

The learning that witnesses thought did take place can be considered to comprise both 'information' and 'understanding'. Thus jurors were considered to have become more knowledgeable about, for example, the role of the EHSSC and about the organisation of general practice, and to have developed some understanding about, for example, why people living in poverty may find it difficult to access services, and the dilemmas associated with balancing local needs and specialist services. For the witnesses the learning process was expressed in terms of their raised awareness of lack of knowledge or understanding among citizens, but also the importance of 'going back to basics' and understanding the points from which ordinary citizens are starting in considering issues of public policy.

When asked about any likely impact on the way they might do their job in future, two of the witnesses returned to earlier reservations about the limited time available for discussion.

Others identified specific points that had been raised that they would want to reflect on. Two witnesses whose jobs involve them in public consultation discussed the possibility of using citizens' juries in the context of other consultation initiatives. Interestingly, both discussed the potential of the model as a way of consulting with different 'target groups', thus using the same approach to hearing and questioning witnesses and enabling time for deliberation, but with groups drawn from, for example, particular neighbourhoods, from particular age groups, or from users of particular services, rather than from a random sample of the adult population. One suggested that this could be a means of increasing the accountability of groups involved in partnership initiatives, while the other was considering the model in the context of service development. He referred to the difference between people who have a knowledge of the subject which comes from direct experience, for example living with mental health problems, and 'the general public' who have no direct experience of such issues and thus who give greater credibility to the views of those who do have such experience. In this context it is of note that when the jurors were asked about witnesses they themselves would like to call, they identified that they would like to call someone who had experience as a long-term user of health and social services and they heard from a woman who is the mother of a child with learning difficulties. The sampling method could have identified someone in this position as a juror – in the context of this exercise she was identified as an expert witness.

As I have suggested above, there is a way in which the allocation of people to different roles within the context of a citizens' jury may obscure the shared identity of all participants as 'citizens'. There is also the potential for different types of 'expert' knowledge to be recognised as having a vital role to play in determining effective policy outcomes. Deliberation between 'experts' and 'ordinary people' may enable the development of awareness that both are citizens with shared interests in the development of more effective public policy.

The potential significance of the jury in building citizenship awareness may have been affected by the particular political context in which the jury took place. At the time this jury was being conducted the people of Northern Ireland were waiting for the resolution of the constitutional situation and hoping that this would contribute to the resolution of conflict within the province based in religious difference. The notion of 'citizenship' had a particular resonance in this context. The response from one of the witnesses to the question 'what does the term citizen mean to you?' was 'a citizen for me represents a goal beyond ethnicity...beyond the tribe formed by family or religion'. This witness suggested that it was a term which referred to the character of civil society which in Northern Ireland could be considered to be only partly formed. For him the notion of 'citizens' deliberating in this way was part of a process through which a more 'civilised' way of doing things could be developed.

The witnesses did identify themselves as citizens and offered the following definitions of what that meant:

A person with rights and responsibilities within a culture/country with which he/she identifies in a way that encourages full participation

Any individual member of the public has the right to be involved to whatever level they wish in matters of public interest

Equality – a right to have a say and be heard, to be responsible for, rights in terms of basic values, to realise their potential, self-worth, self-esteem, not to be marginalised

A person interested in the whole of the community in which they reside. An active participant who is interested in a range of issues and prepared to contribute to that community

Another respondent suggested it was not a term she used and that it sounded more like an American term. However she also suggested that it implied someone who not only lived in, but also participated in the community.

The witnesses' concepts of citizenship included the notion of rights attaching to the status of citizen as well as a concept of citizenship as a practice. There was also a sense that citizenship needed to be forged out of struggle – that it was something to be striven for and thus potentially a more vital concept than in communities where it is less contested.

7. The impact on commissioners and policy outcomes

The commissioners of the Belfast jury shared with some witnesses a sense of the importance of the jury beyond the immediate purpose of exploring citizens' views about proposals for the future organisation of health and social services. As the first citizens' jury that had been held in Northern Ireland it had a broader symbolic purpose – reflected in the response of one of the commissioners that the term citizen meant 'damn all in Northern Ireland' and that it was particularly important to assert the importance of citizenship at the time when the Assembly was in the process of being formed.

In rather different way, the Swansea jury was significant as an experiment in engaging young people in the process of public consultation and thus the response of the commissioner was concerned with the value of the model *per se* as well as to the specific content of the recommendations emerging from the process of deliberation.

The Belfast jury was jointly commissioned by the EHSSB and EHSSC. The Swansea jury was commissioned by the Millennium Debate of the Age. All those interviewed had seen at least part of the jury in action, but only one had observed the entire process.

In both cases citizens' juries were seen by commissioners as a way of accessing the views of people who would otherwise probably not engage in dialogue on such issues of public policy. For the MDA there was the added objective of being able to say that they had included young people within the overall process of consultation. The specific focus of the Belfast jury was seen to be one which required extended deliberation in order to get to grips with the complex issues involved. This was not seen to be an issue which could be adequately addressed by means of a public meeting or through questionnaires. A citizens' jury was seen to have the potential to overcome the tendency to segment consultation and instead engage in a more strategic debate which could also be seen publicly to be independent. The role of expert facilitators was considered important to this process. The opportunity to inform as well as consult was also a reason for MDA choosing this method. The method was also seen by the Belfast commissioners as having the potential to demonstrate to professionals that ordinary people are 'switched on' to the issues and capable of engaging in deliberation about them. One response to having observed the process was that it was salutary for the professionals involved in acting as witnesses to experience a role reversal and that the impact on the attitudes of those who had been part of the process was an important outcome.

The overall responses of commissioners to the two juries were very different. The commissioners of the Belfast jury were very positive about the way in which the jury had been conducted and felt they had got from the process material which they could incorporate directly into their response to the government on the consultation paper. In contrast, the commissioner of the Swansea jury was dissatisfied with the way the jury had been conducted and disappointed with the outcomes of deliberation. While she was prepared to try the method again as a means of consulting with young people, she was looking to very different ways of both structuring and encouraging the process of deliberation. Evidence relating to the deliberative process during the Swansea jury has been considered above and it is important to note that reactions to the reports of each jury were affected by at least some observation of the process. The perceived credibility of the output was related to the perceived credibility of the process and this affected the positive responses to the Belfast jury as well as the rather more negative responses to the Swansea jury.

Dissatisfactions relating to the conduct of the Swansea jury referred both to the behaviour of some young people and to what was seen as the failure of the facilitators to appropriately control this behaviour or to create the conditions in which more positive engagement was possible. Hence one of the main purposes of the citizens' jury was not considered to have been fulfilled – the commissioner saw no evidence of the young people becoming more informed about the issues being debated. But there was also some disappointment at the lack of creativity and imagination in the ideas coming from the jurors. The commissioner suggested that this was partly because facilitators had tried to adapt the process 'on the hoof' when it was becoming clear that they were getting little response from the jurors.

In terms of impact, then, the commissioner felt a number of lessons had been learned, but these were mostly negative – how not to conduct citizens' juries with young people, rather than important insights into young people's thinking about the issue under discussion. Nevertheless there was a commitment to draw on the jurors' report and to provide feedback to the jurors about the progress of the MDA.

The Belfast jury lived up to the commissioners' expectations regarding its composition, and, to the extent that they could judge from having observed only part of the process by which it had been conducted. There was a recognition (shared by the jurors and witnesses) that even in the extended time available for discussion it was not possible fully to get to grips with all issues involved and that a written report cannot adequately communicate the full thinking behind deliberations. Nevertheless there was a comment about how well focused discussion had been and that the discussions had embraced the complexity required.

The commissioners were able to identify a number of key messages coming from the jurors' deliberations which related both to the process of decision making as well as to the content of the debate. For the purpose of this report these can be summarised as:

- messages about the knowledge of and perception of the Board and the Council by the public

- about the importance of localised methods of engaging with the public while also enabling input on strategic issues

- the capacity of the public to identify the significance of 'non service' issues, such as research and medical education, as well as to reflect on issues which make a more direct impact – such as service fragmentation

- the quickness with which people got over their initial reserve and how uninhibited they were in dealing with complex issues.

The implications of jury recommendations were as much to do with how the Board and Council go about public consultation in future as about the messages they should be including within their response to the consultation paper. Thus, while there was a clearly laid out process of responding to the consultation and incorporating jurors' recommendation within their response document, the process of drawing on the citizens' jury experience will continue for some time to come as both bodies consider future strategies for public participation. One direct result is that the jurors will be included on the circulation lists of both organisations and will not only receive information but be invited to contribute to future deliberations. Possibilities being considered included ways in which Board meetings might be made more genuinely open to public input and precise ways in which the jurors might continue to play a role in decision making. The notion of a standing citizens' panel was raised, but there was also an awareness that this would change the jurors as they became increasingly knowledgeable about health service issues. Other decisions had still to be made at the time the interviews were conducted and were likely to be influenced by other factors: the future of the Northern Ireland Assembly and the implications of that for public engagement and decision making processes, as well as more specific decisions about the future organisation of health and social care services and thus the location at which public engagement might need to take place.

In the context of a developing strategy for public participation, citizens' juries were considered likely to have some future role, although all three respondents were agreed that it is a method to be used sparingly. One described the likely circumstances for future use of this method as in cases where there was no feel for what the public preference was and where there was no right or wrong answer. Exploring the values underpinning views or decisions may be as important as the decision itself. Another gave a particular example which could fit that situation: the decision whether or not to pursue water fluoridation.

The jurors themselves expressed very different degrees of confidence that their deliberations would make a difference. More were confident that their views would be listened to than that they would actually make a difference. One said she was more confident that they would be listened to having taking part than she was before they started. Some were very uncertain about either. 'Wait and see' said one. When it came to whether or not the jury and the report would make a difference some spoke of the place of the jury in the overall decision-making process:

> At the end of the day I'm not 100 per cent confident, but I have thought about it a bit. The jury is not a decision making body. There are other factors to be taken into consideration. If our ideas are practical then yes, if they're not too viable it's more like 50 per cent, if our ideas are completely impossible then they will make no difference.

One juror felt the fact that jurors with many different backgrounds had been saying the same thing meant that they would have an impact. Another less optimistic juror said that in her experience decisions would already have been made and that consultation is a sop to the conscience of officials. She suggested that the public should be there when the actual decisions are being made, rather than consulted outside this process.

The young people in the Swansea jury showed a similar range of optimism about whether their views would be listened to or make a difference. Some questioned whether they would be listened to because they are teenagers and some reflected previous experiences of being told their views were important then nothing coming from it:

> *I am quite confident but think that the people reading our report might overlook something because of the ages of the jurors*

> *Politicians don't listen to young people*

> *The people looking at our opinions are probably older and not teenagers, so they may not approve of our conclusions.*

8. Issues raised

In this final section I discuss a number of issues arising from the evaluation and consider what these might imply for the development of the citizens' jury model and for the criteria by which such methods of citizen participation may be evaluated.

Fairness and inclusiveness

The criterion of 'fairness' defined by Webler (1995) as one of the key criteria for the evaluation of methods of citizen participation reflects fairness in access to the process, in determining the agenda and in taking part in the process on an equal footing. The fair access criterion is that everyone who could be affected by the decision reached is invited to take part. In those cases where selection among all those potentially affected is a practical necessity this should be undertaken by random selection. In this section I will reflect on these two juries in particular and on the model in general in the context of the access criteria. In doing so I will suggest that the notion of fairness should also include the concept of inclusiveness.

The nature of the topics addressed by both juries was such that the number of people affected by the take up of jury recommendations is huge. Indeed the Swansea jurors were contributing to a debate which has the capacity to affect the lives and opportunities of people as yet unborn. Selection was thus inevitable in these, as in all citizens' juries. The model is premised on the selection of a sample of citizens and to the extent that random sampling means that all members of the population are equally likely to be included it is a 'fair' approach to selection. However, it is now acknowledged that a group of 16 cannot be statistically representative of a total population and thus the small number of participants suggests some compromise on the principle of fairness in the selection process. The exclusion of people from minority ethnic groups because of the small proportion within the relevant populations is an example of this.

Jurors cannot be considered in any way to be 'representatives' of particular constituencies. They are invited to take part to contribute their own ideas and views, informed by the information they receive during the jury process and by the opportunities for deliberation this affords.

They speak on their own behalf and are not required to be accountable for the opinions they express, nor any decisions they might reach. The issue of jury composition is thus not so much a question of whether or not this meets criteria of either statistical or democratic representativeness, but rather whether or not it meets criteria of inclusiveness. Is the citizens' jury model a method of citizen participation which can include all citizens – whatever their background and current circumstances? And what are the implications for the deliberative process of including a diverse group of citizens who are not only 'perfect strangers' (Sang and Davies, 1998), but who also may have very different styles and means of communication?

The invitation to take part in the juries attracted people who were not especially 'active' in their citizenship, although who, by and large, could not be considered to be alienated from political or civic processes. With some exceptions the jurors themselves regarded their fellow jurors as constituting a reasonable cross section of people living in their area. To that extent the process can be considered to have met the objective of successfully engaging people who might not otherwise have 'put themselves forward' to take part in processes of public consultation. But this is a different criterion from that of 'fairness' as defined by Webler.

There were some types of voices which were not heard directly within the juries. In neither case did the deliberations include people from black or minority ethnic groups or the voice of people living with a disability or of very old people.

Elsewhere citizens' juries have involved a group comprising jurors of different ethnic backgrounds. For example, one of the other MDA juries comprised a majority of black jurors reflecting the ethnic composition of the area. As Webler has suggested if juries are to involve people whose first language is not English and for whom extended debate in English would be difficult, then interpreters will be needed to enable effective communication. But the inclusion of cultural difference is not just a question of 'translation', but of different styles of speech and interaction which have the potential to change the process of deliberation per se. Communication norms vary between different social groups. Assumptions that deliberation is culturally neutral and universal have been challenged by Young (1996) and others. Young has argued that an inclusive model of communication must recognise cultural specificity in deliberative practices. Neither of these juries can contribute to our understanding of how deliberation among groups from different ethnic backgrounds can be enabled. The absence of black jurors also means that the outcomes of deliberations do not reflect the experience or perspective of minority ethnic people. In the specific contexts of these two juries we do not know, for example, how black people might view the characteristics of a culturally-sensitive health service, nor do we know whether black young people would have similar views to those of white teenagers about an urban environment in which different age groups live close together.

The absence of other groups also needs to be considered. None of the jurors identified themselves as having a physical or sensory impairment. If the juries had included blind people or people who are hard of hearing this would not only have meant the inclusion of views and perspectives derived from the experience of living with a sensory impairment, it would also have affected the process through which deliberation could be conducted. Practical arrangements would have had to be made to ensure written material was available to people unable to read this, and hearing loops would have had to be provided to enable deaf people to take part in discussion. Including people with mobility problems would have required attention to be given to accessibility of venues and to the layout of accommodation. For example, the room in which the Swansea jury was conducted was rather cramped and would not have been able to accommodate a young person moving round it in a wheelchair.

The citizens' jury model requires intensive input over a period of four to five days. Both the young people and the adult jurors in Belfast were evidently tired by the end of the process and some of the young people expressed a preference for shorter periods of discussion. Although some people over 70 did reply positively to the invitation this is important again because it may exclude the experiences of a group who may have a different perspective on public policy issues as a result both of past and current experiences. Deliberation between those who have experience of a pre-welfare state society and those who have grown up not knowing the insecurities which preceded this could produce different insights. In the context of the Belfast jury it is of particular significance because older people are proportionately more frequent users of health services.

Finally, while recruitment profiles covered the social class spectrum, it is likely that none of the jurors were among those living in greatest poverty. People living in poverty may see little in citizens' juries which speaks to their immediate priorities and may be inhibited from taking part by the middle class connotations of such a process.

It can be concluded that inclusive approaches to citizen participation require a range of different methods which make it possible for people in different circumstances to take part, and which enable particular experiences to be collectively articulated to inform the overall debate. No single method of participation is likely fully to meet the 'inclusiveness' criterion. Thus, it may not be a problem that the intensity of a citizens' jury excludes frail older people if other methods, such as that developed by Age Concern Scotland in Fife, are being used to enable them to have their voices heard (Barnes and Bennet, 1998). Marginalised groups whose voices have been excluded from decision making processes often need to be able to articulate and define their different and distinct perspectives before engaging in a process of dialogue with more powerful social groups. Some respondents in this study suggested that the deliberative method characterised by a citizens' jury could be used to explore the particular perspectives of sub-groups of citizens on public policy issues – people living with mental health problems, for example. The Swansea jury can be seen as an attempt to do just that, although the experience suggests that a more substantial adaptation of the model would be necessary effectively to engage the interests and creativity of young people. Deliberation can take place in very different forums – using the term 'citizens' jury' to describe all deliberative forums is neither accurate nor helpful. The challenge is to develop a range of methods for participation which, between them, enable all groups to take part in ways which are appropriate to their needs and circumstances.

One of the attractions of the citizens' jury model to public policy makers is that it engages those who might not otherwise take part. One danger in the proliferation of separate forums in which different groups of citizens are engaged in dialogue is that there is a tendency to give greater legitimacy to the 'authentic voices' (Crosby, 1996) of disinterested citizens, than to those who have particular experiences which influence the views they express. There is a danger that a hierarchy of legitimacy might develop which would conflict with the universal notions on which citizenship is based. Another potential problem lies in the fact that one of the objectives of democratic renewal is to enable deliberation between people with different backgrounds, experiences and views. 'The hope (if not always the expectation) is that increasing the proportion of our representatives who come from disadvantaged and excluded groups will challenge and subsequently modify the basis on which public policy is defined. This can occur only in contexts which bring the differences together: where representatives who originate from one group are confronted by representatives who originate from another, and where interaction between them produces something new.' (Phillips, 1995). If there are times when enabling separate deliberation among distinct groups is necessary, it will also be necessary to create forums in which effective deliberation between different groups is also possible.

Experts, innocents and citizen users

People are invited to play different roles; the roles of witness and juror are distinct, although all those who play these roles are citizens. Some of the perspectives of those not directly included within the jury were represented by witnesses. Thus, witnesses to the Belfast jury included a man speaking on behalf of an organisation for disabled people; jurors sought and heard from a witness who spoke as the mother of a child with learning difficulties about the experience of using a range of both health and social care services, while a community development for health worker spoke of the experiences of people living in poverty which related both to health and to health service issues. In Swansea the young people themselves highlighted the importance of designing environments which can include disabled people. Only one Belfast juror identified themselves as the person mainly responsible for the care of children and none identified themselves as the main person responsible for the care of other relatives or friends. None of the jurors identified themselves as a disabled person. But the woman who was called as a witness because of her role as 'carer' of a disabled child could have been sampled from the Electoral Register, as could the man representing the disabled people's organisation. Both are citizens who have general as well as specific interests in issues of public policy in general and health policy in particular. Both could have occupied roles as jurors rather than witnesses. Indeed, the disabled man originally thought he had been invited as a juror and arrived at the start of the jury to take part throughout the process. The presence among the jurors themselves of citizens with impairments, with personal experience of caring for a disabled child, or of growing older and making more frequent and intensive use of health and social care services, could be expected to have had an impact on both the nature and output of such deliberations. In practice people with such experiences acted as 'experts' drawing on their experiential knowledge as a source of evidence to be used by the 'ordinary' members of the public. Similarly, some of the witnesses had experience as citizens of taking part in participation initiatives.

One of the attractions of the citizens' jury model (referred to by witnesses and commissioners in this study and evident in many discussions amongst public officials about public participation) is that it can engage people who have no particular interest in the issue under discussion and who are not members of interest groups. Naomi Pfeffer (1995) has suggested that policy makers seek to consult with 'quasi people' – people who are devoid of previous knowledge or interest in the subject. The perceived unrepresentativeness of those who offer to become involved in citizen panels of user groups is a common theme in research into participation (for example, Barnes and McIver, 1999, Mort, Harrison and Wistow, 1995). Respondents in this study were concerned that continuing to consult with this group of jurors would compromise their status as 'innocents'.

The random nature of jury selection can identify people who might have a special interest (because of their work or their status as a user of a particular service) and thus might qualify as 'experts' or be considered to be 'citizen users'. This might include, for example, people who because of chronic ill health are long term and intensive users of health services. However, such people are perhaps least likely to take part in a citizens' jury and jurors themselves realised the importance of including such experiences within their deliberations. For people who have experienced being marginalised and denied a voice, organisation within interest or identity groups is often a necessary precursor to taking part on a broader stage (for example, Williams and Schoultz, 1984).

There are two issues arising from this discussion which are of importance in considering how deliberation can develop. Firstly, at different times in their lives and in different contexts people may be defined as citizens or experts. Whilst witnesses and jurors play different roles within a citizens' jury both roles are necessary to achieving the overall purpose, and the interests of witnesses and experts will not necessarily diverge. Secondly, a tendency to prioritise the views of 'innocents' or to regard those as more legitimate than the 'unrepresentative' views of members of interest or identity groups may reinforce the comparatively powerless position of those who are members of marginalised social groups. Consideration needs to be given to ways in which mixed groups of citizens can access the experiential knowledge of people in powerless positions as well as the expert knowledge of powerful officials.

Participation in deliberation

The 'fairness' criterion introduced above also reflects fairness in the context of the deliberative process. Others (such as Armour, 1995) have pointed out that the citizens' jury model does not meet the criterion of fairness in determining the agenda since the 'charge' is determined before people are invited to take part. McIver (1997) has described the way in which jury questions have been formulated with input from steering groups and both agendas from these juries were formulated with substantial input from advisory groups. Neither of the two groups of jurors in the juries studied for this evaluation knew exactly what the subject for discussion was when they agreed to take part. In this context the citizens' jury model can be considered the opposite of a community development approach which seeks to enable communities to identify issues of importance to them as topics for participatory action. It is not a model which is designed to start from the concerns and experiences of citizen participants, but to enable citizens to respond to issues of concern identified by commissioners. The nature of the deliberative process in this context is likely to be different from that taking place in forums where the issue for discussion has been determined by reference to the direct concerns of the participants themselves.

There was evidence of very unequal participation by jurors in the plenary discussions, although there were indications that this was, to some extent, compensated by engagement within small group sessions. Lack of engagement did not appear to be the result of deliberate obstruction, but of different levels of confidence in speaking out in a group of this size. While the small group sessions provided an opportunity for input and were welcomed by the jurors, decisions about what was to go in the final report were reached in plenary and thus some people did not take part in the ultimate decision making process.

The notion of informed deliberation among citizens is one which recognises that citizens have knowledge and understanding to draw on in the process of deliberation, but that particular knowledge and understanding about the topic under discussion is needed to provide an additional resource on which they can make a judgement. The 'competence' criterion defined by Webler addresses this aspect of the process. He defines competence in discourse as the 'construction of the most valid understandings and agreements possible given what is reasonably knowable at the time' (1995, p58). He does not suggest that this means that citizens should seek to acquire the knowledge of experts and reach the same decisions as they might do. Rather 'People recognise that expertise is valuable, but they are suspicious that experts may purport a political agenda.' (ibid, p57). The deliberative process in Belfast demonstrated that jurors were questioning the evidence of witnesses and using their own experience and knowledge on occasion to do so. They were debating among themselves the credibility and significance of the evidence with which they were presented. However, both jurors and witnesses were concerned that there was not enough time for them to do this adequately. There was also a suggestion that a 'disinterested' approach to deliberation lacked the authenticity of deeply held views deriving from particular experiences.

It was evident that the young people in the Swansea jury were pleased that young people's views were being sought. But the process of deliberation did not specifically invite them to talk from their own experience about what it is like to be a young person living in the type of neighbourhoods they do and to validate that experience as something to be drawn on in deliberation. This might have assisted them to go beyond the rather limited question and answer process which characterised much of the process of deliberation in the plenary sessions. In the case of the Swansea jury the fact that the topic for discussion was not framed by the young people themselves seemed to be more of a problem than in the case of the Belfast jury. While the general issue of 'living in cities' appeared to be one which could speak to young people's experience, the way in which the issue was framed and structured tended to exclude issues which were of active and direct concern to them. A more open approach in the first instance based in young people's accounts of their lives might have been more creative in this instance. If the citizens' jury model is in part defined by the fact that the topic for discussion is pre-determined, then this model may not be the most appropriate approach to engaging with young people.

The deliberative process in the Belfast jury was more successful in its own right than in the Swansea jury and the Belfast jurors were largely satisfied that the process had enabled differences of view to be expressed. On those topics on which jurors did deliberate in some depth, different views were expressed, different perspectives offered and initial ideas were clarified and distinguished as a result. There was evidence of increased understanding as well as increased knowledge and that this had caused some people to reflect on pre-existing views and to draw different conclusions. Certain jurors took on roles of facilitating others to clarify their views. However, it is not clear how any fundamental difference or conflict between jurors might have been addressed. Interviews suggested that the contributions of two jurors had provoked some feelings of antagonism, but there was little indication of the overt expression of this during the conduct of the jury. The imperative to reach a resolution within a specified time period in the context of a well structured process to cover the range of complex issues raised by the consultation paper may have caused jurors to emphasise consensus rather than difference.

Both juries demonstrated that 'ordinary citizens' can not only respond to issues raised with them by policy makers but can also come up with their own solutions and ideas unprompted by official proposals. They were prepared and able to challenge experts and the preparedness of experts to be honest in the face of challenges was important in developing understanding. The experience caused experts to consider carefully how information could be made accessible for a lay audience and some were reminded just how difficult it can be to avoid using jargon which is inaccessible to many people. The majority of jurors found it a demanding but positive experience and thought that they had learnt from the process.

The impact on democratic practice, citizenship and policy

These findings echo those of other reflections on the experience of citizens' juries (Coote and Lenaghan, 1997, Davies, 1998, McIver, 1997) as well as studies of other models of public participation. What is not clear is the capacity of the beneficial effects of intensive, but short term, involvement to be sustained. The commissioners of both juries felt an obligation to maintain contact with the jurors. In the case of the Belfast jury there has been active discussion of possibilities for engaging with the jurors on future occasions. While some groups of citizens are motivated to make a continuing input to public policy making, others are not. Long term input may be neither possible nor wished for the majority of those who may nevertheless want to be able to take part in some way. But some opportunities for follow up are likely to be important if jurors are not to feel that the experience was an isolated one with no continuing relevance to their own lives or to the decision making process.

The 'goodwill factor' is an important consideration in addressing the outcomes of the jury process. As I indicated in the introduction to this report, the concept of outcome cannot be divorced from that of process and it is important to consider outcomes across a range of potential locations in which these might be felt.

The policy context of both juries was a diffuse one. The Belfast jury was addressing a specific set of proposals, but these were broad ranging and the capacity to act on jurors' recommendations went beyond the scope of either of the commissioning agencies. The Millennium Debate of the Age has long term and diverse objectives which can only be achieved by exerting influence on a number of different public bodies. To look for and expect immediate policy outcomes is unrealistic in relation to both these juries.

In the context of the increasingly high profile given to public participation in the NHS, the Belfast jury has added a new dimension to action already being taken in this respect and has probably played an important role in confirming existing commitments and adding to the argument to persuade those as yet unconvinced. Importantly, the experience of the jury has contributed to an understanding of the role which different methods of engaging with the public have to play in an overall strategy for public participation (IHSM, NHSE, NHS

Confederation, 1998). It has led to realistic assessments of the place citizens' juries may play alongside other methods operating at a more local level and engaging with different sub-groups.

The Swansea experience had a 'back to the drawing board' response from the commissioner in terms of *how* young people might be engaged, but also a continuing commitment to explore ways which might be more appropriate to releasing the creativity of young people.

In the same way as it has not been possible to point to specific policy outcomes flowing from the jurors' recommendations, it is difficult to point to concrete evidence about transformations in jurors' sense of themselves as active citizens. But while 'transformation' may be too strong a word, the experience was a significant one for some jurors in both juries. Most jurors reported that the juries had been important learning experiences for them and there was immediate evidence that most had followed up in some way – at least by talking with others about the experience. Jurors' responses about the significance of an opportunity both to be heard and to hear from others indicates the rather low expectations people have about being able to influence public policy. In both cases the degree of goodwill among jurors resulting from this experience is an important indication of the potential resource to be tapped, but also places considerable responsibility on those commissioning the juries to ensure that this is not turned to cynicism by lack of response.

These are important messages in view of the need for a diverse range of approaches to developing more participative forms of democratic practice capable of engaging different citizens and achieving different types of objectives. The question 'what is the best way of doing it?' usually has to be answered by 'it depends...' That may be frustrating to those looking for a panacea, but it reflects the complexity of the task involved in developing both more responsive public services and a more active polity.

Researching deliberation in practice

The evaluation was not successful in answering all the questions posed, but has been able to reflect the perspective of participants as well as to provide an independent observation of the process. Earlier and closer liaison between researchers and those commissioned to recruit jurors should make it more possible to answer remaining questions about why people do not take part as well as why they do.

Evidence about the nature of the deliberative process and the questions raised about the inclusiveness of the jury model emphasise the importance of comparison between this method of engaging citizens and other methods which can be used to define issues as well as explore them, and which can engage with the particular experiences of groups of citizens whose life experiences may lead to rather different conclusions about issues of public policy. Such comparisons would need to consider both the nature and outcomes of deliberation among different groups.

Reflecting on the findings and the discussion of them, it is possible to refine the criteria by which methods to enable citizen deliberation might be evaluated. Webler's normative yardsticks': fairness and competence, need to be developed adequately to reflect the potential capacity of deliberative methods to engage with diversity and difference. The following criteria might be used to evaluate different models of participation – not to determine which is the 'best', but to increase our understanding of the contribution different models may make to building a deliberative democracy and how to design a strategy using more than one model.

- **Inclusiveness** refers to the capacity of such methods to include any citizen. It reflects both the practical requirements necessary to enable communication between those who use different languages of communication and between those who have sensory impairments and those who do not. It includes their capacity to enable communication between people from different social groups whose communication norms vary. And it refers to inherent characteristics of the model which affect the feasibility of participation by groups in different circumstances.

- **Dealing with difference and dissent.** The greater the potential for inclusiveness the greater the diversity of experience which will be represented within deliberative forums. An absence of dissent is not necessary a positive indicator. Nor is obtaining a consensus output necessarily the only desirable outcome of deliberative processes which are not established to act as decision arbiters. The capacity of deliberative methods to enable difference and dissent to be identified, engaged with and understood may be a more important indicator of their 'success' than whether or not a consensus decision is reached at the end.

- **Scrutinising experts and information.** This refers to the capacity to enable non-experts to question and challenge traditional sources and holders of knowledge and expertise. It is a vital part of the process of ensuring greater public accountability and necessary in any attempt to shift the balance between expert and citizen decision making. It also refers to the scrutinising of the notion of 'the expert' per se. Do deliberative methods enable different types of knowledge and expertise to provide a resource in the process of deliberation?

- **Developing skills and understanding.** The key purpose of deliberation is to achieve change. Change will only come about if people develop new ideas, new ways of looking at the world, new understandings. Thus a criterion for evaluating deliberative methods is whether or not the process enables the participants to learn through taking part.

- **Producing an outcome.** All those who take part hope that this will make a difference beyond the forum itself. While direct cause and effect may be difficult to pin down, and the timescales in which change might become evident fall outside the funding periods of evaluative research, changes in the type of policy decisions reached and in perceptions of the health of the democratic process are longer term indicators of the collective impact of citizen deliberation. There is an assumption that including people previously excluded from decision-making processes will add a new dimension to the decision-making process. We need to know whether this is indeed the case, and if not, why. Do officials select only those recommendations they agree with? Does increasing involvement lead to co-option?

Interest in the practical development of new ways of involving citizens has been accompanied by a wish on the part of those investing in such processes to know if they worked and if they made a difference. Chapter 1 suggested that evaluation in this context needs to go beyond asking whether it worked, to recognise that perspectives on success will often be different depending on the position of those making the assessment, and that understanding the reasons for success or failure is essential if evaluation is to be understood as a process of learning rather than judging. The criteria suggested above do not lend themselves to straightforward tick box analysis, they cannot be answered by yes/no responses. They require an analysis which is more appropriately understood as a process of 'researching' rather than 'evaluating'. There are still questions to be answered about the nature and impact of new opportunities for citizen deliberation, but to answer them is likely to stretch the concept of evaluation beyond its limits.

Afterword: Evaluation, democracy and deliberation – a report of an IPPR seminar
Clare Delap

Introduction

This evaluation was commissioned in the wake of a huge rise in innovative methods of public involvement accompanied by increasing endorsement from central and local policy-making bodies. At the forefront of this move has been the development of 'deliberative' methods: citizens' juries and workshops, consultative panels, deliberative opinion polls, are all in the public limelight.

Their widening practical application begs some questions about judging the success of methods which claim to have both democratic implications and policy outcomes. Do such methods produce what they set out to do? They also raise issues about the relative merits of different models of involvement. What criteria can be used to compare their effectiveness?

A number of practitioners have begun to assess the impact of these innovative methods of public involvement. In November 1998 IPPR brought together those with direct experience of commissioning, assessing and practising new methods of public involvement to discuss the questions raised by Marian Barnes' draft report. The aim was to examine recent strategies for evaluation, explore the creation of criteria for success, and look at the policy implications of evaluation. There follows a report of the key points of the discussion[6].

Features of Marian Barnes' evaluation strategy

The evaluation described here builds on a number of recent attempts to evaluate citizens' juries and related methods of involvement (McIver, S (1997) Armour, A (1995) and Hall and Stewart (1996)). The strategy adopted by Marian Barnes differed from previous work in a number of ways.

● **A focus on the deliberative *process*:** This evaluation strategy attempted to assess the nature of interaction during a specific deliberative event in a particularly intense and systematic way.

Seminar participants noted that this detailed examination led to a set of conclusions about group discussions comparable to other small group meetings such as American town meetings.

- **A focus on all the *individuals* involved:** Evaluations of citizens' juries carried out in the UK so far have mainly concentrated on the public bodies who have commissioned the consultation and their use of juries in policy formation (McIver, S (1997)) Marian Barnes assessed the impact on all those involved in the jury including 'expert' witnesses and attempted to evaluate from the perspective of the participants. It was agreed that the decision to assess the impact on all those involved in the jury including witnesses added to our knowledge of deliberative processes but discussants argued that the impact on policy was of primary importance.

- **A limited timescale:** The author has commented that the timescale of the evaluation limited the scope of her assessment of the impact of the two citizens' juries. Participants at the seminar discussed the trade-offs between the relatively low cost of this evaluation strategy and losing the opportunity to evaluate the longer-term impact.

The approach used and the results of the evaluation led to the examination of the purpose and nature of citizen involvement and highlighted the need for further research in areas identified below.

Participation and representation

A long-running debate about the process of recruitment and the nature of the participants at deliberative events surfaced during this seminar (Delap, C 1998). It was argued that decisions about how to treat the results of such exercises were partly dependent on the extent to which the participants were a representative sample of the population. It is important to know whether particular viewpoints are being over-represented or whether some sections of the population are being favoured while others are denied a voice. Some participants disagreed saying that citizens' juries, like many other participatory methods were an attempt to bring a group of lay people into a decision-making process and that exact representative samples should play a relatively minor role in assessing their success.

Marian Barnes had decided to concentrate on what kinds of people were or were not at the juries she evaluated. This was one way of circumventing the argument about representativeness but the central issue about the selection process remains a key debating point in assessing the merits of different methods of participation. If the purpose is to reach conclusions about what the public would think given time and information, then it is important to know the nature of the sample of people chosen. If the principle purpose is to bring an informed 'lay' perspective to a decision making process, then the issue of representation is less important.

Where does deliberation begin?

In this evaluation the process of deliberation was central to the assessment of the model. However, there were questions raised about concentrating on the four days of the jury and on those present. Some participants were concerned that the preparation of juries and related methods was key to perceptions about their outcomes. How is the charge or question set? How is the agenda constructed? In many of the citizens' juries that have taken place the dialogue between different kinds of citizens begins long before the jury event, when an advisory group is recruited consisting of stakeholders and experts in the subject. It was argued that these stages were just as much part of a citizens' jury process as the event itself and should also be subject to evaluation.[7]

Assessing the impact: how long and for whom?

It was unclear when the evaluation of a citizens' jury or similar event should start but it was widely agreed that a key area for future research and evaluation must be the longer-term and wider impact of the event and the decisions made. Participating in deliberative events has an immediate and significant impact on those taking part but how long does it last and what about the wider community? It was also pointed out that effects of participation exercises were extremely diffuse. One representative of a local authority explained that a key outcome of the citizens' jury held by her organisation was to bring about major change of attitude within the authority leading to a wider and longer-term strategy of public involvement and open decision-making.

This has implications for the subjects of the evaluation: who should be interviewed and assessed? Marian Barnes has included witnesses and individual representatives of commissioning bodies in her evaluation, but what about those involved in the planning of a jury or those who were part of the organisation who held the consultation?

The effects of an event such as a citizens' jury on the wider community has not been documented here or elsewhere. But there was speculation about how participatory exercises were perceived by the wider public. Recent research into public consultation discussed at the seminar showed that the public were likely to be suspicious about the representative nature of participatory events and sceptical about their impact (Lowndes, V, Stoker, Prachett L et al, 1998). Some participants wondered about the legitimacy of the results of two juries being held on the same subject with contradictory results. Others argued that the legitimacy of such public involvement exercises depended on how 'fair' and open the construction and organisation were perceived to be. It would be valuable to identify criteria for the success of public involvement exercises from the perspective of those members of the population not taking part as well as those actively involved. Different mechanisms for consulting or involving lay bodies evoke differing perceptions of trust and legitimacy: whether or not the results of a survey are seen as legitimate is different to the legitimacy credited to the decisions reached by a legal jury for instance.

Enhancing democracy or enhancing decision-making?

Participants at the seminar stressed that in order for a consultation exercise or strategy to be judged a success its purpose should be clear. Is the aim to improve the quality of decisions being made about services, thus improving the delivery of those services? Or is it to enhance democracy and/or improve the legitimacy of local authorities? One discussant suggested that if the aim was to improve the quality of decisions made, participation could be a double-edged sword: opening up the decisions to more people may undermine the role of elected representatives and it also may complicate rather than improve the decision making process; he was wary of making governance unwieldy through too much consultation. Other participants argued that more debate and involvement must be a sign of a healthy democracy and that it was a positive indication of the amount of interaction between representatives and the public.

This led to a debate about the relationship between representative democracy and participation. Viewed from the point of view of organisations representing the public, participation could be seen as a way of making more effective decisions. For many it is fundamental to the act of representation. Most participants agreed with John Stewart and others that representation should be a continuous process of interaction between the elected and the electorate (Prior, D, Stewart, J, Walsh, K (1995)). It was also argued that participation was a component of democratic justice. Individual citizens have the right to participate actively in a democracy and every time they take part in a consultation exercise they are exercising that right. They are also taking on some of the responsibilities which come with decision making.

Conclusions: Evaluation and future research

The seminar stressed the need to see single acts of participation such as citizens' juries as part of a strategy and a philosophy. As some of the key questions about the nature of democratic participation had still to be addressed, many discussants called for more research before methods into specific exercises could be determined. For those actively practising involvement exercises, however, the need for monitoring is always immediate. It was agreed that some of the criteria identified by this and other evaluations were valuable but that the next step must be to examine the goals, nature, and effects of widening participation.

Endnotes

1. The notion of 'expert' is itself open to different interpretations. It is used here to refer to anyone who has particular knowledge relevant to the issue under discussion. As we will see, this can include those with experiential knowledge as well as with professional knowledge.

2. The proposal to introduce primary care groups (PCGs) into the English health service was a key feature of the White Paper *The New NHS: Modern, Dependable*. PCGs will have responsibility for commissioning health services for populations of approximately 100,000, and are thus intended to bring commissioning closer to what were referred to in the White Paper as 'natural communities'. GP fundholding is discontinued and all GPs will become members of a PCG.

3. Data collection instruments are available from IPPR.

4. In line with the profile of the area eight jurors described themselves as Protestant, six as Roman Catholic, and two said they had no religion.

5. Whether this be older people unable to leave home without assistance making new friends as well as developing confidence that they can make a difference to services after becoming involved in user panels (Barnes and Bennet, 1998), or women with mental health problems working together to find their own solutions to their problems (MIND, 1986), the potential enjoyment and value of working together is an important factor affecting the success of any participation initiative.

6. The seminar was chaired by Anna Coote, the King's Fund and PIP. The speakers were: Marian Barnes, University of Birmingham, Roger Jowell, Social and Community Planning Research, Shirley McIver, University of Birmingham, Gerry Stoker, University of Strathclyde, Paul Whiteley, University of Sheffield, Jenny De Ville, Lambeth and Southwark Health Authority. Participants were from local and health authorities, central government departments, consumer and user organisations and academic and research institutions.

7. Smith and Wales argue that the initial preparatory stage to a citizens' jury is crucial in assessing its integrity as it forms part of the deliberative process (forthcoming, 1999).

References

Armour A (1995) 'The citizens' jury model of public participation: a critical evaluation' in O Renn, T Weßler, and P Wiedemann (eds) *Fairness and Competence in Citizen Participation. Evaluating Models for Environmental Discourse* Dordrecht, Kluwer Academic Publishers.

Barnes M (1993) 'Introducing new stakeholders: user and researcher interests in evaluative research' *Policy and Politics* vol 21, no 1, pp47-58.

Barnes M (1997) *The People's Health Service?* Birmingham, NHS Confederation.

Barnes M and Bennet, G (1998) 'Frail bodies, courageous voices: older people influencing community care' *Health and Social Care in the Community* vol 6, no 2, pp102-111.

Barnes M, Hall D, Leurs R, McIver S and Stewart J (19970 *Citizen Participation: A Framework for Evaluation* Occasional Paper 11, University of Birmingham, School of Public Policy.

Barnes M, Harrison S, Mort M and Shardlow P (1999) *Unequal Partners: User Groups and Community Care* Bristol, The Policy Press.

Barnes M and Wistow G (1993) *Gaining Influence, Gaining Support: Working with Carers in Research and Practice* Leeds, Nuffield Institute for Health.

Beresford P and Harding T (eds) (1993) *A Challenge to Change: practical experiences of building user-led services* London, National Institute for Social Work.

Cooke J, Ide M, Pittard A and Swain L (nd) *The development of an evaluation methodology for advocacy projects working with older people* group project assignment, MA in Applied Research and Quality Evaluation, Dept of Sociological Studies, University of Sheffield.

Coote A and Lenaghan J (1997) *Citizens' Juries: Theory into Practice* London, IPPR.

Crosby N (1995) 'Citizens' juries: one solution for difficult environmental problems' in Renn O et al (ibid)

Crosby N (1996) *Creating an Authentic Voice of the People,* Paper presented at the annual meeting of the Midwest Political Science Association.

Davies S (1998) '"It changes your life": the citizens' jury from the juror's perspective' in Davie S, Elizabeth S, Hanley B, New B and Sang B (eds) *Ordinary Wisdom. Reflections on an experiment in citizenship and health* London, The King's Fund.

Delap C (1998) *Making Better Decisions: Report of an IPPR symposium on citizens' juries and other methods of public involvement* London, IPPR.

Dryzek J S (1990) *Discursive Democracy. Politics, Policy and Political Science* Cambridge, Cambridge University Press.

Dunkerley D and Glasner P (1998) 'Empowering the public? Citizens' juries and the new genetic technologies' *Critical Public Health,* vol 8, no 3, pp181-192.

Fetterman d M, Kaftarian S J and Wandersman, (eds) (1996) *Empowerment Evaluation. Knowledge and Tools for Self-Assessment and Accountability* Thousand Oaks, Sage.

Finne H, Levin M and Nilssen T (1995) 'Trailing research: a model for useful programme evaluation' *Evaluation,* vol 1, no 1, pp11-31.

Gastil J (1993) *Democracy in Small Groups. Participation, Decision Making and Communication* Philadelphia PA, New Society Publishers.

Greene J C (1996) 'Qualitative evaluation and scientific citizenship: reflections and refractions' *Evaluation* vol 2, no 3, pp277-89.

Gutman A and Thompson D (1996) *Democracy and Disagreement* Cambridge (Mass), Harvard University Press.

Harrison S, Barnes M and Mort M (1997) 'Praise and damnation: mental health user groups and the construction of organisational legitimacy', *Public Policy and Administration* vol 12, no 2, pp4-16.

House E (1993) *Professional Evaluation* London/Newbury Park, Sage.

IHSM, NHSE, NHS Confederation (1998) *In the Public Interest: developing a strategy for public participation in the NHS* Leeds, NHSE.

LGMB (1996) *Citizens' Juries in Local Government: Report for LGMB on the Pilot Projects* London, Local Government Management Board.

Lowndes V, Stoker, Prachett L et al (1998) *Enhancing Public Participation in Local Government: a research report* London, DETR

McIver S (1997) *An Evaluation of the King's Fund Citizens' Juries Programme* University of Birmingham, Health Services Management Centre.

Means R and Smith R (1988) 'Implementing a pluralistic approach to evaluation in health education' *Policy and Politics* vol 16, no 1, pp17-28.

MIND (1986) *Finding our own solutions: women's experiences of mental health care* London, MIND

New, B (1998) 'Citizens' juries: empowerment, self-development, informed view or arbitration?' in Davies et al (1998) op cit.

Pfeffer N (1995) 'What the NHS needs are quasi-people' *The IHSM Network* 2(2), p1

Phillips A (1993) *Democracy and Difference* Cambridge, Polity Press.

Phillips A (1995) *The Politics of Presence* Oxford, Oxford University Press.

Prior D, Stewart J, Walsh K (1995) *Citizenship: rights, community and participation* London, Pitman.

Rebien C (1996) 'Participatory evaluation of development assistance: dealing with power and facilitative learning' *Evaluation*, vol 2, no 2, pp151-71.

Sang B and Davies S (1998) 'Facilitating a citizens' jury: working with "perfect strangers"', in Davies et al (1998) op cit

Skelcher C, McCabe A, Lowndes V and Nanton, P (1996) *Community Networks in Urban Regneration* Bristol, The Policy Press.

Smith G and Cantley C (1988) 'Pluralistic evaluation' in *Evaluation* , Research Highlights on Social Work 8 London, Jessica Kingsley.

Smith D, and Wales C (1999 forthcoming) 'The theory and practice of citizens' juries' *Policy and Politics*

Stewart J, Kendall E and Coote A (1994) *Citizens' Juries* London, IPPR.

Stewart J and Walsh K (1994) 'Performance measurement: when performance can never be finally defined' *Public Money and Management*, vol 14, no 2, pp49-50.

Stringer E (1996) *Action Research. A Handbook for Practitioners* Thousand Oaks, Sage.

Sullivan H (1997) *Evaluation of the pilot devolution projects in Birmingham* University of Birmingham, INLOGOV.

VanderPlaat M (1995) 'Beyond technique: issues in evaluating for empowerment' *Evaluation* vol 1, no 1, pp81-96.

Voluntary Activity Unit (1997) *Monitoring and Evaluation of Community Development in Northern Ireland* Belfast, Department of Health and Social Services.

Webler T (1995) '"Right" discourse in citizen participation: an evaluative yardstick' in Renn O et al (1995) op cit

Young I M (1996) 'Communication and the other: beyond deliberative democracy' in S Benhabib (ed) *Democracy and Difference: Contesting the Boundaries of the Political*, Princeton.